# WHEN THE MASK DROPS

## What Is Behind Narcissism?

Shabina

**BALBOA.**
PRESS

A DIVISION OF HAY HOUSE

Balboa Press books may be ordered through booksellers or by contacting:

Balboa Press
A Division of Hay House
1663 Liberty Drive
Bloomington, IN 47403
www.balboapress.com.au
1 (877) 407-4847

Print information available on the last page.

ISBN: 978-1-5043-1252-3 (sc)
ISBN: 978-1-5043-1251-6 (e)

Balboa Press rev. date:  03/05/2018

# ACKNOWLEDGMENTS

I wish to thank my mum for being a very positive, brave and strong woman. She truly believes that only unconditional love can turn any situation around. I wish to thank my dad who is a very courageous, determined and compassionate husband and a father to 4 children. I couldn't have asked for better parents.

I wish to thank my husband who has given me this opportunity to explore my own theories and my 3 beautiful children who are my true inspiration. Together they have taught me lessons in life as a mother, mentor and a friend. My brothers and my sister who are my real backbone because we have no secrets.

I wish to acknowledge all my heroes and these are the real gifted healers in this world. Without them my journey into this world would have ended way before I started writing this book 10 years ago.

# CHAPTER 1

*"What maintains a relationship, is being brutally honest"*

T HE MAN THAT was once the love of her life, the man she cherished with all her heart, the lifelong partner, her confidant, whose presence made her heart quiver with excitement, the smell that would drive her to ecstasy now feels like something out of a very long dream. That abundance of love, the exuberant, luscious and fuzzy feeling of boundless love is now replaced with the numbness, the numbness that is travelling around the body, felt in many different parts of the body that is now chewed up feeling like a tasteless and over chewed gum, lustreless and lifeless is perhaps, beyond repair.

The thoughts are floating in Narissa's head while she is sitting on an old wooden bench under the solid oak tree in the park not far from home, in fact just a few blocks away.

It was a warm sunny Sunday afternoon and all the three grown up children out of the house on their own errands, a husband who is walking around the house in a grumpy mood again, Narissa took herself out for a walk with Bronco. This was a great little escape where she sometimes came to clear her head. The sun is bright today, the sky is blue and there is a light breeze. Bronco, is running around the park smelling everything as he moves, wagging his tail whenever he lifts his head momentarily and catches glimpses of Narissa, whom he adores. Bronco was only a tiny little pup, 6 weeks old when the family got him 8 years ago. He was an extremely cute little pup and he wouldn't leave Maddie's arms and so the family had no choice but to bring him home. With his black spots on white coat, tiny little legs, he was always the smallest dog in the park but a very brave one. A Jack Russell cross Chihuahua, Bronco was the perfect little addition to the family, so we all thought, except Lawrence. Lawrence, was sometimes a heartless man, had no empathy and treated animals as if they didn't have a soul. He would yell at Bronco for no particular reason.

How we all despise him sometimes, thought Narissa.

After 30 long and laboured years of this relationship, Narissa is walking like a lost sheep looking for pastures green and sweet, full of juice to quench her thirst and fill her up with substance abound.

Twenty minutes' walk down the path is a house with 3 grown kids and a father who hates them all, so it seems. There is always some reason to argue. The kids on their own are fine and get on well together, most of the times. It is a different story when their father is around. You wouldn't believe that he was their biological father. 'What's the whole point of a relationship where you always feel alone?' Narissa cannot seem to take her mind off the analysis that is twirling in her head like burning fumes from a pan of overheated oil, making you cough and gag.

Right now she cannot express this numbness which cannot be explained without sounding like a psychological damaged individual. All she knows is that she has woken up to understand that the emotional thread that once felt strong and unbreakable was an imagination that was entwined in the word LOVE.'

Narissa's thoughts won't leave her alone. Besides what else could she do now?

'How emotionally far away we are from each other. The distance feels so icy as if suffering from a frost bite. No one can feel the chilliness, the loneliness and the distance...only I can. The mould growing inside me from so much coldness is spreading fast and it doesn't feel healthy. It feels rather toxic and I can often feel it spreading like cancer cells. The thoughts just keep coming and Narissa momentarily forgets where she is. Narissa has developed a nasty pain in her liver and spleen area. She feels bloated even if she hadn't eaten. The pain can be sometimes unbearable but she cannot utter a word of discomfort to her husband of 30 years. The whole abdominal area feels tight and bloated, yet she eats healthy. When she burps she can feel the bitter acidy taste floating up her oesophagus, much like the bitterness she feels inside when she thinks of Lawrence.

His comments makes her cringe. "You are putting on weight, must be happy huh? I think you need to exercise." He points out very amiably.

Narissa takes a deep breath and the air that enters her nostrils feel cold and it smells of death, icy and tasteless. In fact Narissa has smelt death a few times.

'The closeness that existed once is now lost somewhere, like losing an earring in the forest loaded with the tallest pine trees you can imagine, engulfing you, smothering you in darkness, and all you hear is the rustling of leaves that give you no support, only more loneliness.'

The darkness that is engulfing her right now is unbearable.

'I know I will not find my jewel in this smothering darkness and as I walk further into the forest I feel more alone than ever. Alone in my journey, I hope to find something that will bring the blue skies and sunshine back to my life, to add that sparkle into my hollow life. What will it take?' Narissa is getting too deep into her thoughts.

The separateness she shares is beyond repair, so she feels and yet she has a little light of hope in her deepest crevice of her heart that there might be a slight chance that her relationship with Lawrence may change, one day. He might just become a caring man.

'What a load of nonsense!' She thought out loud.

'I am an optimist and I see positive in everybody and everything in life. I have the ability to change every negative situation into a positive one. I will keep smiling no matter how difficult or painful a situation is. After all, I am the only one who can change the way I feel.' With that thought Narissa is feeling a bit sleepy now. She is feeling a bit heavy in herself as she does when she has these moments.

Bronco's bark makes Narissa sit up. She didn't realise she had been slouching on the park bench as her thoughts were drowning in her head. Bronco is running as fast as a race horse and he looks so happy. He is coming with something in his mouth. Looks like a shoe. Bronco drops the shoe down right next to Narissa's feet and starts smelling the inside of the shoe.

Narissa snapped out of her thoughts as she has to give her attention to Bronco. She darts her eyes around the park and can see the beauty of the trees around her, the crimson colours of the Chinese Tallow, yellows and browns of the birch, the purple brown colours of the maple makes the landscape more desirable than her life.

'How did we get here to this platform of penurious moment of our lives? What is marriage all about, an institution, or is it really a heavenly act upon which blessings are showered as two become one? Is it truly where two people start sharing everything and start thinking for one another and living for each other with respect and dignity? This journey of two people staying in a bond forever is a long winding journey like an intestine twined in the viscera of our stomach and our journey becomes a peristaltic movement in a world full of distractions. The catalysts and enzymes are our friends, family and society which contribute to the making or breaking of this perilous bond.' Whoa! That was a lot of analysis in split seconds, thought Narissa.

"What have we got here, Bronco?" Narissa asks, bending down from her seating position and caressing Bronco along his spine from the head to the back.

Bronco just looks up with his pathetic puppy love look, wags his tail and coos at Narissa. He blinks and licks his lips, writhes along the grass and makes himself more comfortable, getting closer to

Narissa. Narissa knows he loves her very much, as much as everyone else in the family except sometimes, Lawrence.

'Love in a marriage is expressed in many different ways, the intimacy that starts off cautiously, then boundaries are broken with years gone by, becomes a handful when two become too comfortable in each other's space. When to give space and when to enter the space, when to back off and when to blend in, is a horrific experience. There aren't any models or rules and all it takes is a bit of common sense, maturity and awareness.'

'A commitment from two people to love each other unconditionally, support each other in good times and in bad, to love and respect each other and be the rock for each other. A lifelong partner who will be with you in your emotional journey. The physical touch, the immense exhilaration of experiencing the expression of deep love from the core of your heart muscles and every single vein and nerve of your body, sending you to ecstasy is just exuberant! The true expression of love can only be experienced in a relationship that has all the elements of trust, loyalty and honesty. Growing together mentally, emotionally and spiritually and keeping that bond alive. Expecting changes, unexpected situations but remaining true to self and to your partner is what makes a marriage work.' Narissa is full on back into her thoughts.

'The biggest problem is created when 2 individuals digress in different directions, whether it is in career or in self growth, of which both are important part of our lives. This change which is about growth, inner spiritual growth in the form of career growth, intellectual growth or personal growth helps us to have a fulfilling, meaningful life, can be daunting if your mind is blocked and if you think that a person must not change at all. However, nothing in life is permanent and change is inevitable.' Narissa is trying to make sense of her life and her journey, especially after getting married and having children.

'It's this important change in growth that becomes unacceptable to some people.

In some cultures though, marriage is merely tying two people together for the sake of copulation. The off-springs are created to take over family heritage, pride and keep it rolling generations after generations. Living in such a matrimonial bond becomes a habit. Is marriage then just an idolised life or is marriage supposed to tie people together out of love?'

'I must be getting home', Narissa thinks to herself and tries to get up slowly. It seems the sun is fast descending over the horizon. Narissa looks at Bronco and he is still having a good time with the shoe. The tatty old shoe obviously was buried somewhere, thought Narissa. Judging by all the soil stuck to it and the age of it.

"Let's go home, Bronco." With that command, Bronco immediately gets up and wagging his tail in excitement drops the shoe and waits for Narissa to put him on his leash. He is very good like that. Bronco looks up and listens to Narissa's commands. Watching a happy face like Bronco's always energises Narissa.

The walk home was in silence with Bronco just walking close to Narissa obediently.

Approaching the driveway to the house, Narissa starts to get quizzy in her tummy because she can never know what to expect when she leaves everyone at home with Lawrence.

Narissa opens the gate and lets Bronco off the leash. He runs to the back of the house. He must be thirsty. Walking around the house to get to the back door, Narissa is listening in, just to be sure that she is not walking into an argument. Usually the argument is between Lawrence and Maddie, because Maddie won't tolerate injustice of any sort and also because she was the first born. Not hearing any shouting or yelling, she walks briskly around the side path with its overgrown lemon tree, mandarin tree and the honeysuckle vine hugging the fence, with Bronco trying to pee at every tree, Narissa enters the backyard. The backyard is big enough to create space for everyone. A little haven Narissa created with willow in one corner of the yard stretched across a pagoda with its beautiful purple blooms flowing down made a pretty setting. A rusty old bench seated under the willow where Narissa likes to sit and read or just lie in the sun was her idea of solitude, which she hardly ever got. With three children 2 years apart and a husband who mostly acted like a child didn't give her that privilege. A trampoline tucked away in the other corner which no one uses except for maybe Ella sometimes; a vegetable plantar box with few silver beets and the herb plantar with rosemary, chives, oregano, mint, chillies and parsley. Max's basketball hoop in a little courtyard and the clothes line to one side of the fence with some overgrown Rhododendrons and sweet pea tree made a cosy backyard. Thank goodness for all the trees, they dampened the noise the family created.

This is where the kids hung out the most when they were little. There was a swing set and a small sand pit but they have all been replaced with lawn now. Bronco loves rolling in the grass and his toys are scattered all around the back yard.

His dog house which is under the patio is in a cosy corner but it looks like he has taken his smelly blanket out of it.

Entering through the sliding back door Narissa can see Lawrence through the French door separating the kitchen and the family lounge, which he is sitting on his favourite recliner lounge chair watching sports. This is Lawrence's life and he likes to fill his days just lazing around. She can see the back of his head and only the top but she can see him enjoying himself as he is bouncing up and down with excitement. As long as he is happy all is good, she thought. Except with Lawrence you never know. His mood changes without any warning.

Narissa glances towards Lawrence again, who can't see her as he is busy enjoying some game on TV, the man she had married thirty years ago, the man who showed her that love was real. She was only19 and he was 24 when they first met. Lawrence was a real gentleman. They used to go dancing to the nightclubs, dancing the night away in each other's arms. She knew he was the one. She couldn't look at another man in this way ever! Whenever their eyes met, she would see the spark which was a direct link to her soul. The spark would send undulating waves from her throat down the digestive tract and produce massive amount of nostalgia. Suddenly the throat would dry up and the butterflies would fly into her stomach, whirling around and what she was feeling was neither happiness nor anxiety. This mixture of emotions were quite unpleasant and forge Narissa into uttering words that she thought she wasn't capable of. The body reels itself inside like it wants to entwine itself around his body.

Lawrence and Narissa hooked up whenever they had a moment of solace from studies, work and friends. She wanted to be with him 24/7. She loved his smell, the big flat palms of his hands engulfed around her small body frame and making her feel secured, special and amazingly enough, on top of the world. She felt she was the only person on earth who actually knew what love was. Looking around the beautiful green lustrous, perfectly manicured lawn at the university campus, you will find young lovers sprawled around, dead to the outside world. In the library cubicles you will hear wisps of whispering couples, whispering words of love. In the canteen you will see couples feeding each other their lunch that has gone cold while couples have been looking into each other's eyes forgetting that they have purchased their food or in each other's arms, kissing, cuddling and embraced in a sea of love. This is such an enchanting period of life in any young adults' life. Her love was special.

Yet she was so independent, carefree and enjoyed life to the fullest. She was so much in control of herself, her life. Narissa was a good looking, popular girl, had no problems getting boyfriends not that she was ever interested in men then, till Lawrence appeared in her life. She was getting more hits than her friends who were always envious of her and had to make excuses for her whenever she was asked out on dates, because Narissa was never available. Narissa considered herself to be an average young woman who knew how to be herself. She was fun loving, enjoyed life to the fullest and without getting into deep troubles.

Movies, little excursions together to the ski slopes, mountain climbing, canoeing down the river, restaurants, and garden trips made it an exciting time of her life with the love of her life and she had no reason to think otherwise or to doubt that she could ever be alone in this relationship. Lawrence was with her all the time. She just had to ask and he would be over to help her out.

The part-time job working at the local cafe had helped pay for the extracurricular activities while juggling studies at university and work was pretty good. Narissa was able to do it all. Partying was part of life at University and there would be some event or party every Friday or Saturday night. Some young adults really wasted themselves on booze and were non-functional for the entire weekend, what a waste! Narissa spent her evenings working and clubbing after finishing work. Girlie parties, playing with makeup and having a few glasses of champagne on a Saturday afternoon was an occasional treat.

When Narissa met Lawrence, he was the hunk with round buns and his biceps were solid as, oh what a guy. Everyone thought he was a great catch. The way he looked at her, just made her feel like a marshmallow melting in a cup of hot chocolate. If you stirred a bit, she would disappear. His warmth radiated around her like a cocoon and she was protected from all the wild animals out there. That feeling of warmth and fuzziness, like being in her mother's womb was just so comfortable. She was mesmerising about this guy she had met at a friend's house.

It was a cold wintry morning and Narissa was rushing out of the cafe after her morning shift, a very early start of 6 am, rushing to catch the bus to university. With her bag over her shoulder, wearing black T-shirt, jeans and shoes fit for running, her long spiral permed hair flying around her face covering her vision momentarily, she swished her head left and right to get the glimpse of the traffic so she could step on the road and make it across to the other side to catch the bus, she stepped on and off the road several times and then suddenly, she was seeing faces over herself.

Lying on the footpath with legs stretched out, one on the footpath and one on the road, must be the cycling lane because she hadn't been crushed by traffic yet. She tried to pull herself up, but her back hurt. At least I am still alive, so she thought, because she can see faces and she can feel wet jeans and her palms feel wet from the wet leaves that are covering the kerb. Wholly crap! Narrisa realised that she had slipped and fell, even with a pair of good running shoes, the few inches of height difference between the road and the footpath with wet rotting slippery elm leaves gave way to her body.

Several people tried to help her get up and she could hear people saying "don't move her!" She felt like jelly on a plate and whilst people were trying to get a grip on her body, her arms and legs flopped like wobbling jelly on a plate.

"Do we call an ambulance?" People are now gathering all around me and Narissa began to feel suffocated and dizzy. She tried to get up again and slipped on the rotten slippery elm leaves again.

"I have to catch the bus. I have a lecture to attend." Narissa managed to speak out. People are now helping her get up. Gees, does it take 50 people to lift a small body? I don't need their help, thought Narissa. She was a very strong girl always lifting heavy boxes at work, moving furniture around when she didn't have anything better planned, in her tiny little bedsit that she lived in.

"I am ok guys, seriously. Thank you everyone." She is now in half sitting position and burst out laughing. Just looking at herself with rotten wet elm leaves that formed a cushion for head that prevented major head injuries, hanging off her long spiral hair and palms of my hands covered in black brown muck, she just had to laugh at herself.

"She is going into shock." Someone was heard saying.

'I seriously have to get rid of all the clowns around me, thought Narissa and with that she shook herself up and bravely lifting her hands up in the air, "hey, I am alive!" Still laughing, quickly made a quick mental check of all her limbs, her arms are good, twirling her fingers and found none broken. The legs are fine but the back hurts a bit.

"Thank you everyone. I now have to catch the bus which I believe I have missed, so if you will excuse me, I have to make a run."

People are clapping, "yay, she will be fine." I heard someone say behind me. A gentleman in a black suit with a fancy tie with his arms stretched out gestured that he will guide me to cross the road. The headstrong person I was, I declined. "Thank you sir, but I have to do this on my own for my own self. Sorry." I gave a millisecond smile, just a gesture of politeness.

Narissa stepped on the road with no oncoming traffic, walked halfway across the road when she heard people clapping and cheering. OMG! Big deal. Must be my arse, she thought. A lot of her friends told her that men love watching the way she walked. She didn't know that because she had never seen her own back side before and wasn't even sure what to look for.

With a smile on her face Narissa got to the other side, turned around and gave a small bow and waved with one arm as if she was some entertainer finishing an act.

The crowd dispersed slowly and that's when she saw Lawrence again. He was the quiet guy standing at the rim of the crowd and as the crowd dispersed, he stood there starring at her. He looked small and vulnerable as if he wanted to say something but missed the opportunity. She had seen Lawrence at the cafe several times and he was always alone. This is the guy she had seen at this random person's house, actually a friend of a university friend where she accompanied the friend to pick up some books.

The bus arrived, blocking her vision and she hopped on, brain switched back to university mode and now her focus is on her lecture with wet jeans that will take ages to dry due to the low winter sun, at least she is on her way.

Narissa kept working at the coffee shop to have some pocket money to travel and buy small items of luxury for herself. Even though her parents supported her financially for tuition, the part time work paid for the electricity, gas, rent and food. She needed money for clothes and some outings as well. Living in a small flat close to university gave Narissa the freedom from her parents who were out of town suburban dwellers. They were hard working and that's probably where she got her inspirations from to get a good education and be an independent woman. At age 18 not many people wanted to move out of home due to expanses. In Narissa's house her parents being in high powered positions didn't leave much room for exciting things to do. This gave her all the good reason to move out and live in an inner city apartment close to university.

Narissa can't recall exactly when and how she started dating Lawrence. She had finished her Bachelor of Education and was job hunting when Lawrence proposed to her. She accepted once Lawrence met her parents. Most of the boys she dated didn't last long and Lawrence was the only one who let her be herself, laughed at her jokes, complimented her all the time and made a point of visiting her family. Lawrence was the only guy who seemed genuinely interested in Narissa and her interests. There was a quick engagement and not long after was small wedding ceremony witnessed by family and very close friends. Lawrence had organised everything and he just told her what was happening. Narissa was madly in love with him. His smooth charming and ever so caring nature made her feel extremely special. He had eyes only for her. Lawrence was always on time whenever they were out on dates and called her every day to tell her how much he loved her and there was no reason to fault him. He was amazing in bed too. His touches would send electrifying vibrations throughout her body, his moves in bed were smooth as silk and she was sent to ecstasy every time.

Now, 30 years on Narissa can't stand him in bed. He snores, he rolls over pulling sheets down, duvet down and makes too much noise in the bed. She has no energy, no mood or desire to be held like madly in love any more.

These days she is on fire, ready to explode as if some firecrackers were thrown in to her. At the first sign of a spark she is on full fire. Even the smells are revolting. Who buys his after shave now? I am sure it was a cheap gift from some family member. What the heck is he wearing in bed, feels like a sleeping bag, the thoughts are transferring a negative vibration into her body.

Mind you she herself at one stage had to resort to grandma style pyjamas. Narissa remembers those breast feeding days, when she had to put a pad to stop the sheets getting wet from the milk that flowed profusely at the slightest squeeze. Before than there were sexy slinky silky nighties or even birthday suit. Can't wear G-strings any more as the backside looks like a big blob of jelly.

Narissa has put on kilos but she doesn't know how. She relentlessly cleans, tidies the house, runs up and down the stairs, in and out of cars, carry all the heavy groceries and yet she feels like a big blob. The whole stomach and hip area has tightness like a wet rope that cannot be untangled. The bloatedness in the stomach reminds her that she was pregnant once and the inflexibility surrounding the female organs and viscera provide a very unsexy feeling.

Things have changed too much for her to be turning around. Sometimes her eyes are filled with tears but they dry out even before they have the chance to drip down past the bottom eyelid. The crying is only inside and the sobs are released as little sighs.

'Whatever happened to the infectious love I felt once? What has happened to our commitment to each other?' She thought.

She told herself that she knew how to make marriages work. Her friends used to discuss how to keep marriages alive and how not to lose interest in your partners. Narissa thought she had it all under control.

Some marriages couldn't keep the sparkle but some seemed to know how. Narissa was one who knew how to have it all, because she used to give her friends some really good advice on how to keep their marriage alive. It is all about respecting each other, the physical space and the mental space. Added to this the importance of going on a date every once in a while and keeping a busy schedule juggling work life balance, but never losing interest in your spouse.

In her case, however she married a man she didn't quite know. She thought she knew this person whom she had dated for 2 years before tying the knot. She is beginning to doubt herself and him. She knew a lot of effort is required to keep the marriage active. Her grandmother used to give her tips and advice. It takes two to tango. 'Why does it feel like I am alone and my love is not reciprocating at all? All I know is for some reason I am questioning everything about this marriage and it freakin hurts!'

Narissa pushes the door and slowly makes her way inside the kitchen. "Hi, everyone, I am home."

No one replies. Narissa walks to the oven where her roast is cooking. She has a whole chicken roasting in there, a tray with potatoes, sweet potatoes and pumpkin. Now she has to put the fish on which she had already marinated and then she has to steam the vegetables. Dinner will be ready.

It seems obvious that someone had emptied a packet of Doritos and dropped some bits on the floor but never thought of cleaning up. The kitchen sink has dishes piled up and it wasn't how she had left this place, some 30 minutes ago.

The clothes are still on the line and apart from clothes hanging on kitchen bar stool and dishes piled up in the sink, nothing much has changed.

Maddie must be home as Narissa can hear her radio on full blast coming from her room.

Being the eldest, Maddie has a big room which happens to be downstairs next to the study. Maddie loves her own space and because she is much disciplined in herself, going to bed at the same time each day and an early riser, it made sense to put her in a room away from the rest of the family. At 24 Maddie is now working full time and gets tired at the end of the day. So on weekends she sleeps in and tidies her room, washes her clothes, sometimes cooks her own meals, comes and goes as she pleases.

Thank goodness for her idea of having a roster set up on the fridge door so Narissa knows who will be home for dinner. The rest of the meals everyone takes care of themselves and life has become a lot easier.

Max, the second child now 22 has become a bit of a loner. He only goes out occasionally. He is trying to finish his degree in

Political science and had joined some activist groups. He has settled down a bit now, thank goodness.

Ella at18 and first year at university is still very indecisive. She has no idea what she wants to do but seems to enjoy fashion and design.

Looks like Max is studying and I can hear his girlfriend in his room. She has been a great help in motivating Max to stick with his studies.

Narissa feels somewhat proud of her children but not with her own self.

*"Loving you doesn't hurt me. The only thing that keeps on hurting me is the fact that you'll never love me back"*

# CHAPTER 2

*"We develop courage by surviving difficult*
*times and challenging adversity"*

'WE CAN'T EVEN talk to each other without having a fight.' As soon as the garage door opens, Narissa cringes. Lawrence is home and that means she has to check what mood he is in. Is he going to complain about work, or all the kid's shoes at the front door or Narissa parking her car too far to the left?

Lawrence's complaining is something Narissa should be used to by now but she is not. It sends her into spasms and sometimes she shivers and begins to feel real tiny.

'Have I got the house tidy, clean, dinner ready, clothes washed?'

The check list races through her head as if she is on a roller coaster, bracing herself. Her shoulders rise up with tension, a twinge in her head makes her lose control of herself and her scapula begins to hurt.

First thing he will do is yell at whoever crosses his path in the house. He will pick on anything and anyone, for little things like having left dishes on the dining table, sitting in front of the TV or computers, chatting on face book. But what was his problem? His life is just work. Is he jealous of everyone just being themselves, in the comfort of their own home? Is chilling out a bad thing?

Narissa wonders why her attitude towards Lawrence has changed so much. She doesn't feel so happy when he comes home for the fear of being told off again.

Narissa had to be a grown up and embrace motherhood when the first child was born. Once upon a time Narissa was a young, vibrant, independent, career minded girl but today she is a mother of three young children. She became a wife and embraced the challenge of being a wife. It was not easy living with someone when you had lived most of your life on your own. The other challenge was not being able to cope with Lawrence's mood changes.

Sometimes Narissa felt like a piece of furniture in the house. 'Is this what I am worth today?' She thought, while picking up bits of Lego and putting them into the box.

Narissa had changed her job to suit the family's lifestyle. In fact to suit Lawrence's ideal belief that a woman's job is looking after the children, the house and the husband. The husband's role is merely to earn the money. Had Narissa known all of this before getting married, she would never ever have gotten married to this douschebag. The anger she feels inside is making her have heartburn.

When Narissa was dating Lawrence she was very vocal. She had expressed her disgust at men who disrespected women, treated them as objects and made them their door mats. Lawrence would just listen and all the time Narissa thought he was agreeing with her, with his occasional smiles. Maybe Lawrence didn't quite understand what Narissa was saying. Maybe he just never thought of himself as one of them. Besides, he didn't show Narissa this side of him at all. Not till the children arrived in this relationship or maybe before but she didn't take much notice, being a person who always saw the positive side to everything.

Looking back and thinking what it would have been like if she had gone to Dubai to teach. One of Narissa's friends went to UK and got an offer to join a research programme in Education. This meant after 18 months of solid work she will have a Doctorate in Education. They had talked about this at University, both keen to

to Narissa that a man of his calibre was not interested in planning for their future together, but she was blind, blinded by the love.

Since they didn't have enough money for a deposit she decided to go for a house and land package which allowed them to save money towards a deposit. So while the house was being built Lawrence and she would be putting money into an account with the building company. For a $2000 deposit they could secure their first home.

Narissa thought buying a house was a great investment. Plus it was making her feel rather warm and fuzzy inside. Imagining what it will be like to decorate their bedroom in her own favourite colours, the dream furniture for their lounge and dining, the kitchen utensils and the list just grew day by day. The excitement felt real even though it was just her imaginations.

They met with a mortgage broker who showed them how they could get into their first home and since they were both working and didn't have any other commitments, they should look at investing into more properties later on. Exactly what Narissa had been saying to Lawrence for a while, obviously falling to deaf ears.

Narissa was getting really ahead of herself and was going on and on to Lawrence about having their first house and then a few investment properties before having children so they will have a solid foundation for them to build their family on, meaning investments so that they could survive on one income when she stayed at home with their children.

Lawrence seemed to agree with everything they had discussed the day before or earlier in the week but changed a few days later.

Lawrence had problems with every single agent they met with. "Narissa, can you not see, that bloody agent was acting like a smart arse and the way he looked at you? Disgusting!"

It was obvious that Lawrence didn't want to work with him.

Narissa found another agent and he was very well presented. Lawrence came up with the same old excuse.

"You can't see, can you? The agent is getting too personal with you." He said.

'Seriously? Nevertheless, why would that bother Lawrence so much? She didn't see or feel that any agent had the hots for her, but who cares? Besides why should that be a problem? Nevertheless, Lawrence should have felt proud to have a hot wife, shouldn't he? He knew that Narissa only loved him and had never given him reason to believe otherwise. It seemed Narissa had to justify herself with Lawrence in everything she did. She had to prove her love for him by making more sacrifices than she had ever done in her life.

Besides, she wasn't the flirty type. When she was on a mission, she meant business.

Lawrence was not one for taking on big projects. He needed a lot of assurance from his mum and friends. When it came to making mortgage payments, buying furniture and refurbishing the house, Lawrence would totally freak out. To solve his money problems, they made a joint account so Lawrence could see how the bank balance was climbing, which he really enjoyed watching, but at the same time find things he could spend on. Narissa was managing all the outgoings and making sure they had enough saved up for a rainy day, and credit cards were always paid off before the interest period came into effect. He had a love of spending especially if it was somebody else's money including his company car which he would drive everywhere and fruitlessly run to the shops several times in a day. He would never plan his day or his requirements for the day and make one trip to get all the chores done. He couldn't prioritise his chores either. Sometimes, Narissa felt like she was a mother to him and had to constantly remind herself that she was his wife and her role and purpose were very different to his requirements.

Narissa and Lawrence furnished their first home with a lot of pride. Even though at the back of Narissa's head she didn't want to shelve the idea of going on her overseas experience, she lived in the present moment and went all out sparing nothing.

Lawrence splashed out on the furniture. Anything that Narissa liked, Lawrence would go and get it. Sometimes Narissa just wanted to sit back for a few days before making a decision but Lawrence didn't. She liked to look extensively before making any decisions when it came to buying furniture, because Narissa believed that you buy once, you buy good quality. Lawrence didn't mind spoiling Narissa like this, not that she minded it at all. They were both working and money coming in and Narissa was clever enough to put some aside in a savings account even though it didn't pay much interest. That didn't matter, it was there if they really needed it.

They had the garden sorted and everything was coming up good. The house was beautiful.

When Narissa told Lawrence about this offer she had received from the university in Bristol for an 18 month Post graduate programme, he got wild. The first thing he said was "what am I going to do?"

"You can find a job easily with your skills. Can't you?" She thought he would love to accompany her but she was so wrong. Immediately he told her that she could just go on her own leaving everything behind.

"We can rent our house out. That's what people do." Narissa didn't want to sell their house since they had only built it a year ago. This opportunity wouldn't come again, she thought to herself.

How wrong was she to think she had full support from Lawrence when they had married? The happiest moment of her life when she loved the man she adored. She thought the world was her oyster. She had understood his love in a different way.

How and why did he change so much? Before getting married he was a lovely man, really paying her a lot of attention, telling her that he loved her cooking, loved her honesty, loved her adventures of life and her free spirited nature.

Lawrence loved her commitment to everything she undertook. He was all over her and she felt totally supported back then.

Lawrence had lied to her. He told her that he had made contact with the embassy and they were looking into things. He also told her his friend was looking for a job for him in the UK. Whenever,

Narissa approached Lawrence on this subject, he just wouldn't say anything. He will walk away or look at her like 'stop nagging me'. She also pulled away because she didn't like pushing people. Narissa wanted Lawrence to be happy with the idea as well. She couldn't think of hurting the man she once adored. She couldn't just walk away and hurt him. It was something Narissa would never do. If she didn't have his support, then she wouldn't go and how will she start all over again when the house they had just purchased a year ago had her money tied there too.

The process was easy for Narissa. All she had to do was accept the offer and then get a letter from the institution which she had to present to the embassy to get a student visa. She didn't see any problems with that, but obviously Lawrence did. She told Lawrence that she will get paid for the work she was going to do but they may have to live on a small budget for a while as she was going to be like a student.

She really wanted Lawrence to accompany her. 'We will have fun travelling together during my breaks,' excitedly she tells Lawrence. The adventurer she was, nothing was impossible for Narissa. Her grandmother always said, 'little sacrifices and hardship pays off so never let an opportunity go by especially if it feels right in your heart.'

Narissa realised that all the changes and commitments were making Lawrence feel very insecure and that's what the change was. It was the responsibility that had made him curl into a deep dark hole. Also, perhaps Narissa was moving far too fast in life. Lawrence needs a lot of time to assimilate information and absorb changes.

As time went on, Lawrence was getting more and more possessive of Narissa. He wouldn't allow her out of his sight either. She was unable to visit friends or talk on the phone for hours as she used to with one of her friends and even just have a coffee with a friend was impossible. Lawrence would drop Narissa to work, pick her up every day and would accompany her to the grocery store and won't even allow her to drive by herself to visit her family.

to finish and decisions had to be made. Narissa was firm and told Lawrence that she was going to book needed to take his passport to make the bookings.

Lawrence had nothing to say and that meant it was all good. Bookings made and paid for made Narissa really excited about this trip. They had 5 nights at two destinations and 3 at the other two, with airport transfers and breakfast included. When the travel time arrived, Lawrence was getting anxious. Narissa didn't know what the anxiety was about but it felt very uncomfortable to be around Lawrence.

Lawrence had packed his entire wardrobe, so it seemed. Narissa talked with him and described each country and what they will need. She helped him sort out his suitcase and got organised for the trip. As the departure date approached, Lawrence was extremely agitated. The week leading up to the trip, Lawrence was hurried, gulping his dinner in few seconds flat and was getting angry with Narissa for no reason. Isn't going away a happy time? He was a handful at the airport, checking his watch 50 times, pacing from one seat to another, checking his tickets a million times, making sure he got the right gate. Narissa had to leave him for a bit because she didn't know what to do. While she was window shopping, Lawrence crept up behind her and immediately started telling her off for looking at expensive T-shirts. "You can get cheaper elsewhere." He shouted at her lifting the price tab up to her eyes as if she couldn't see.

"I am just looking. I am not buying. Calm down" Narissa replied.

When she looked up at him, he was staring at her looking down at her with glassy eyes filled with anger.

"Lawrence, I am just having a look around!" Narissa explained calmly speaking with clenched jaws and raised eyebrows.

Narissa just needed a breather. Lawrence was making her very nervous. To soften the heaviness around Lawrence, Narissa showed him some boxers which had really kinky prints, with smiles and elbowing him affectionately, to break his anger. He wasn't amused.

The airport felt stuffy with millions of people with kids, bags and in wheelchairs. She thought perhaps Lawrence was feeling claustrophobic so she suggested they parked themselves near the window and watched the planes. Bit more spacious and away from the busyness and hustle bustle of the airport lounge.

On the plane, Lawrence was very careful with his luggage making sure no else took his bag space in the overhead compartment. Lawrence liked things in a very specific way. His cabin bag should be just above his seat and every time someone else came in to open, he would jump and tell them it was his bag. It was a bit funny at the beginning. Narissa whispered to him, "Honey don't worry, and relax. The bag will be there. You sit back and listen to music or you can read this book I got for you."

Lawrence talked continuously about all his work stuff and it is usually bad anyway. He complains about everyone and Narissa sometimes switches off. She couldn't tell him to stop because Lawrence gets offended easily. He would tell Narissa how rude she is and that she didn't care. What really bugged Narissa is it is ok for Lawrence to keep talking about his work problems but Narissa can't talk about hers. Anyway, after all his moronic lashing out, he fell asleep.

On arriving at the airport, Lawrence got extremely excited. He was just running fruitlessly looking for a trolley. Narissa grabbed his arm "Lawrence, we have someone from the hotel picking us up and they should be standing with our names on a card." Lucky Narissa spotted a man with their surname and hotel name on a card and they had a trolley for them.

Lawrence won't stop bragging about himself to the driver. The driver just asked one question, "What do you do for a living, Sir?"

While in Singapore, we had a lovely time.

Lawrence enjoyed himself very much and just wanted to buy electronics, clothes and eat. Narissa wanted to explore and take some sightseeing tours and do a bit of touristy things as well. Narissa managed to take some great pictures with her small camera. Lawrence was hopeless with a camera. He could never get the angle right or cut off the head. Nonetheless, he tried.

Narissa's ambitions of owning a camera that could take wide angle pictures and long distance with clarity were crushed a long time ago. She had planned to save up for a good camera and started visiting camera shops to get herself acquainted with different brands and features. When she mentioned it to Lawrence one day, he was also very keen and assured her that there was a great camera shop near his work and he knew someone who worked there who could arrange a good discount for us. Narissa was really excited but it never happened. Lawrence was either lying to her or holding her back from buying a camera, for reasons unknown to her or he was being selfish. Narissa wasn't allowed to go on her own to buy.

She gave up on the idea of getting a good camera for herself but invested in a small digital camera, still a great camera.

On their return from the first trip away, Lawrence raved on to everyone in his family how great his trip was which he had booked and decided to book it all this way so he won't waste time and he managed to strike a really great deal. Narissa was stunned as he never mentioned her at all. Everyone thought Lawrence was such a clever person and struck an amazing deal. His sisters and his parents were full of praise, treating him a little child and giving him all the attention to inflate his ego even more.

Narissa decided that it was time to face motherhood and suggested to Lawrence that they should at least try to conceive, an idea which freaked Lawrence out. Narissa wasn't getting any younger and also she wanted children of her own. She loved children and had a great fascination with the developing mind and that's one reason she was always reading books on mind and body connection, and trying to understand people's behaviour.

It didn't take long after her initial suggestion, Narissa found out that she was indeed pregnant. Challenges became more of a nightmare during the first pregnancy for Narissa. The challenging moments hadn't faded with Lawrence. In fact he seemed to want to run away from all the fuss. Sometimes Lawrence was physically present but emotionally not present. Narissa tried to talk to him about life after baby, how things will change for her, for them both, not just financially but socially as well. Although it always seemed like Lawrence was grasping what she was saying, but often he wasn't. The freaky part was when she was in a situation, he will yell at her for being in a situation as if she had purposely created difficulties for herself, or he will look uncomfortable as if unaware of what to do or how to react. It seemed that Lawrence always needed someone to tell him how to react or to make himself useful.

Lawrence cannot see things clearly, for him to know something he has to experience it. Even then he doesn't always learn from experience. He wants to control everything as if he is the lord almighty.

Maddie, their first child went to full term and while Narissa was very heavily pregnant with her, she ended up having a lot of water retention. Narissa researched a lot on herbal teas and creams to help her to relax and take care of itchy skin eruptions. Sometimes she would feel a bit restless and very uncomfortable and all she needed was someone to hold her and assure her that everything will be alright, just a little rub on the back to comfort her, which Lawrence didn't seem to understand at all. He just couldn't care less. He would just walk around the house looking like he was busy and that Narissa was on her own. Her aches and pains just fell on deaf ears. She had water bottles, herbal teas, and baths and massaged herself on the areas she could reach. The backaches got worse, so bad that Narissa went out and bought some pillows to help her sleep better. Sometimes she would just cry with the pain. She couldn't talk to Lawrence about her discomforts at all because if she tried his response was not pleasant. "You are obsessed with this thing!"

'Maybe I was obsessed with this baby growing inside of me. I can't ignore it as my stomach kept growing bigger and bigger, so I stopped talking to him about the baby. I really wanted some sexy photographs of my expanding tummy but I couldn't ask Lawrence. That would have made him really cross.'

She tried to get Lawrence involved and preparing him for this soul that was about to arrive in this world and showed him the baby followed the guidelines provided at the ante natal classes they had attended. At the class Lawrence always paid attention, asked heaps of sometimes unnecessary questions and made what looked like a lot of effort to learn. Lawrence liked drama and he made a big deal out of everything, like folding nappies. A simple task, he was able to make it tough and it was obvious that he was doing the attention seeking behaviour.

Maddie was born after very long 18 hours of labour. Narissa was exhausted but in all the photos, Lawrence looks the worst. Narissa was up several times during the night at the hospital which felt cold and in the dark of the night, she felt alone. It was just the baby and herself in a ward, by themselves. The tiny little but healthy baby was now lying in a bassinet next to her. For some reason it felt very strange and lonely. Narissa wanted to hold her, kiss her and cuddle her all night. Narissa managed to get some sleep as she was exhausted but felt a bit lonely now that this baby that was once a huge part of Narissa was now out of her and being her own person. She was no longer part of Narissa's body. An emptiness engulfed her once again in the darkness of the night. Why couldn't Lawrence just stay a bit longer and hold her and just allow her to cry? Doesn't he understand what Narissa is going through? The emotions were running high for the new mum. Lawrence didn't have anything else to do at home so what was he rushing home for?

Two days was enough in the hospital. Narissa couldn't wait to get home and rest her bundle of joy in the pretty bassinet she had prepared for the baby, to lie in her own bed and sing to her baby. The cards and flowers were flowing at home from the school and parents who had knitted pretty neutral coloured booties, bonnets and cardigans, the neighbours, family and friends. Narissa didn't want to know the sex of the baby and everyone was curious to know what she had. People were all guessing and wanted to know if they were right. Lawrence had not mentioned once about all the flowers she had received at home and the cards she had received.

The lack of support from Lawrence was even more enhanced

when Narissa experienced helplessness after Maddie's first lot of vaccinations. After the vaccination, Maddie wouldn't settle down. She didn't have any help as Lawrence didn't want any of her family to be involved with their child rearing, instead Narissa ended up calling the help line.

"Hello, can you state your name and address please." This young inexperienced operator answered the phone. 'I couldn't even state my name which I used to proudly announce once, while waiting at tables. I just melted down, telling them that I was alone with this baby who wasn't settling down and I was much stressed. The operator asked me again to state my name.'

What difference does it make, why the heck do they need my name. "Can you please help me or not?" I hesitantly asked.

"Ma'am is there anyone else at home?"

'Why the fuck would I call them if there was someone else at home?'

To that I just blurted out in my rudest voice ever "No! No one is at home. I don't freaking know where my husband is and I have my baby who has been crying all day and sleeping very little after her vaccinations this morning. Should I be worried?" I spoke each word stretching it out so she could understand me fully and not ask me this again.

"Ma'am you are telling me that you are at home alone with a baby who hasn't settled since she had her vaccinations, is that correct?"

"Yes!" I shouted.

"I- I haven't rested all day nor eaten all day and I am exhausted."

"Could you call upon a friend or a relative who could allow you to take some time out and just hold the baby for a few minutes while you rest?"

"What about the baby? Is this normal? I called the medical centre earlier and they advised that I gave my daughter some Pamol and just let her sleep. But it doesn't seem to do much. I am worried for my baby." I am fully crying by now, sitting on the edge of the bed watching Maddie lying on her side as they had advised me to and not letting my sight waiver at all.

"Look, you both need some rest and if you can call upon a friend or relative or just wait for your husband to come home, and let them take charge for a little while, it will help. If you have any further concerns, please call us back. Your baby should be fine by the morning. What your daughter is experiencing is not related to vaccinations at all."

Hopeless, I thought and I put the phone down. By 7pm I was exhausted with Maddie at 6 weeks old, now having projectile vomiting, running a fever and I was feeling tired and weak.

Narissa had called Lawrence at work and he had brushed her off "just go to the Doctors. I will come when I can."

Maddie slept for a bit and she called the nurse again. Suggestions were to give her Pamol and warm water if required. Both Maddie and Narissa were up and down most of the night. It was 3 am and still no sign of Lawrence.

In the morning, Narissa could hear Lawrence taking a shower. He came out with smiles and that made Narissa more furious with him.

With dark black blue bags under her eyes, Narissa felt totally wiped out. The look of exhaustion on her face with her floppy body would have given anyone the indication that Narissa needed some help today. Lawrence wouldn't register all of that anyway, he was just blind to normal human life. He will never acknowledge how she was actually feeling. He only wants to know you when you are ready for him in bed for sexual activities, which clearly Narissa was not, so he smiles and walks around pretending that he hasn't seen her state at all, making Narissa more furious.

"Where were you last night?" she asked furiously. "Maddie had her first lot of vaccinations and she was really very unsettled. I had such a difficult time with her all day and all night. You said you were coming when you can."

"We had our party and the boys decided to go out for drinks.

What's wrong with that?" Lawrence speaks to me like I am some sort of a bimbo.

"Drinks? Coming home after 3am? You think I am stupid?"

"You could have told me that you were going out for the night and had no intention of coming home! You are a liar!" Narissa is feeling really emotional and could do with a hug. Lawrence just stands there starring at her. "Well, all looks fine to me." He says.

She threw a pillow at him and asked him to leave. "I don't want to see you right now. Just leave me!"

"Your choice to have children" and he walks out of the bedroom door.

'Seriously? Did he just say that?

Did I just do that? Threw a pillow at him?'

Narissa exhausted and feeling so weak, so unsupported and so lonely that if it wasn't for Maddie's innocent smile, she might have just gone into deep dark hole called depression. Narissa had to make herself get out of bed for Maddie, to feed her and hold onto her like her precious life.

Lawrence was staying out at work longer and always complaining about funds. Narissa wasn't even going out anywhere, movies, dinners, coffees, clothes had all stopped for her. She was aware of the fact that there will be tough times financially but had never imagined such emotional times. 'What did he do with my savings though?' she thought.

After a year's maternity leave, Narissa was contacted by the school and started on some part-time work. After 10 months of juggling work and raising Maddie on her own, since Lawrence decided to stay at work longer hours, she decided to quit. Narissa had to deal with all childhood illnesses herself, watching all the milestones herself, making decisions on where to send Maddie for pre-school etc. Lawrence was not approachable at all. He didn't want to know about anything. Narissa reluctantly handed in her resignation, mush to the dismay of the Principal, her colleagues and the parents who had gotten so fond of her.

Life returned to a lot more of a normal shape once Narissa gave up her work which she missed dearly. Narissa was able to take Maddie to playgroup, swimming lessons and dancing. Maddie was a clever little girl full of curiosity and was a lot of fun. She picked up words of songs very quickly and was a joy to have around. Maddie had a great passion for reading and would like mum to read the newspaper to her. Sometimes Narissa would skip the words and just give her the gist of the news.

"Mummy, but there are so many words and you only gave a short story. What do all these other words say?" Maddie asks curiously pointing to all the articles in the paper. Maddie is too clever and there is no way I can lie to her in any way.

Narissa was forever cleaning, tidying, cooking, washing and gardening. As well as being a mother to Maddie she became a mother to Lawrence, who just enjoyed his freedom from all the chores around the house.

Narissa thought it was time to have another child so Maddie will have company as well. Having a brother or a sister will help in the long run. Sure enough, a few months later Narissa found that she was pregnant with child number two.

She was so happy, over the moon. I will get to stay at home and enjoy my time with Maddie. A sibling for Maddie, perfect!

She told Lawrence that evening when he was sitting after dinner watching TV. Narissa still had to do the dishes and put Maddie to bed who liked to be read to each and every night. Lawrence didn't participate in any of the chores at home. Lawrence didn't have anything to say. He just folded his lips, clenched his jaws and didn't even look at Narissa. It hurt Narissa to see him like that because she really wanted Lawrence to be part of the growing family. 'Doesn't it give him joy to see his daughter skipping around singing nursery rhymes and trying to show off to her dad? Isn't he curious as to what Maddie does all day?'

It seems that Lawrence thinks Narissa is diseased. He won't come near her and he won't cuddle her. She has to approach him all the time. Each night after dinner, he sits in front of the TV and then moves on to his computer, spending hours each night. For Lawrence home is a place to eat and sleep. Narissa felt like telling him that this isn't a hotel where he can come and go as he wishes and that she isn't his mother.

Maddie in bed and now Narissa can go downstairs and tidy up the kitchen, prepare for the next day, make a cup of tea, shower and perhaps read in bed for a bit before falling asleep.

While coming out of Maddie's bedroom, Narissa could hear giggles. Giggles of a woman. 'Is Lawrence having an affair?'

Narissa was shocked and horrified but hurt at the same time. The mixed emotions made her freeze right outside the study door. She doesn't like to listen or pry on other people's business, unlike Lawrence, who would open her mail if it was from an unknown source, much to her disgust. She couldn't imagine why anyone would do that. Narissa stopped, thinking Maddie should be asleep but the giggles are of a grown woman. She stood outside Maddie's door which was right next to the closed door of the study and heard this woman say "so where is she?"

Narissa ran down the small dark hallway with the street light shining through the small window on the landing and ran to her own bedroom. She flopped on her bed face down, both her palms of her tired hands covering her face and she sobbed. She was feeling so low, that she was having thoughts of running away far far away from everyone in this world. The humiliation was killing her. 'What am I supposed to do? I have a baby and another one on the way and my husband is having an affair?'

She was feeling light headed, throat suffocating her, closing up so no words can come up, chest feeling heavy and stomach feeling acidic she sat up in bed. First thought was, Maddie and the baby. 'My priority is my babies. I can't let anyone or anything affect them.' She sat up, wiped her tears, lifted her head up and made her way to the kitchen.

Narissa started on the dishes. She had a pile of dishes to load and some handwashing to do as well.

'Lawrence could have helped instead of chatting to some low class shit!'

She hurriedly loaded the dishwasher, wiped down all the benches, the high chair and cleaned up the mass that Lawrence had created in the lounge. Newspapers strewn around, a cereal bowl on the coffee table. Lawrence had this habit of eating cereal after dinner sometimes. Narissa put the dirty towels in the laundry and then hurriedly swept the floor. She prepared Maddie's bag for the next day, making sure her swimming gear, towel and goggles were in it. She raced to her room and jumped in the hot shower. She melted down in the shower, crying her heart out. While running around doing the chores she had forgotten about Lawrence's affair but now in the shower her emotions are coming back. 'How could he!' She felt like screaming her lungs out but didn't want to wake Maddie up nor the neighbours hearing her.

She had a long hot shower and got in her bed. 'I will ask him when he comes to bed', she thought.

Narissa must have fallen asleep waiting because she woke up to the sound of the shower at 7 am, must be Lawrence. While lying in bed she felt very small and ugly inside. She just wanted to die. She had to get through the day for Maddie's sake.

'What if Lawrence was having an affair? What was she to do? Where will she go?'

This made Narissa feel sorry for herself. Her tears were streaming down the right side of her face, which was turned against the bathroom door. She didn't want Lawrence to see her tears, at least not till she was ready to confront him.

Narissa was getting bigger with the second baby on the way and sometimes feeling uncomfortable in the morning, really needing to pee. She rushed to the main toilet as she didn't want to face Lawrence in their tiny ensuite bathroom, in case he smiles, that wicked smile which always made her think he was covering up something. Lawrence spends hours in the bathroom as if he is a bride, never been able to understand how or why a man needs so much time in the bathroom, in front of the mirror gawking at himself. Even when they were going out as a young couple, he would get in the bathroom first and usually after an hour, Narissa would try to get in, have a quick shower and as she is putting her make up on, he will barge in and ask her to hurry up. After a few years of being quiet about it, she snapped at him one day, "you moron! Are you so blind that you can't see, I have only been in the bathroom for barely ten minutes and you think I should be ready? You have been in here for over an hour! Fuck you! You selfish moron!"

Narissa went to Maddie's room and she was already up, playing with her Barney soft toy. She was talking to Barney and singing to him, dancing around, so happy. Narissa couldn't walk into her room with a sad face. "Good morning!" Narissa is racing into her room with arms spread out knowing that Maddie will come running to her. She slouched down on the cushioned fluffy carpet and sat on her knees. Maddie is so sensible "don't want to squash the baby inside, mumma." She hugs and kisses her mummy affectionately.

"Look, Mumma, I have made space in my bed for my baby brother. He can have all these toys but all these ones are mine", waiving her arms around in circles to show Narissa the different piles. "Only sometimes we will share."

Narissa loves the way Maddie is so accommodating with her little sibling already. She is absolutely adamant that they were having a boy. Narissa told the Radiologist at the time of the ultrasound that she didn't want to know the sex of the baby. Maddie had gone with her and said she knew it was a boy. Lawrence had refused to go with her telling her that he couldn't take time out of work. "It isn't important, is it?"

'What is important, Lawrence, I sometimes wonder.'

Lawrence was walking to the kitchen and getting breakfast. Narissa tries not to approach him on anything when Maddie is around. If Narissa approaches Lawrence on anything that he dislikes it just boils into an argument. At the same time if she ignores him then he thinks he can get away with it all. Lawrence doesn't know how to discuss matters or talk about anything in a civilised manner. He would rather just ignore everything.

Narissa feeling very uncomfortable has a suspicion that he will try to ignore her for the rest of the week by staying at work till really late. 'I think that he knows that I was outside the study door long enough to hear this woman he was chatting with on his computer.'

The week was long for Narissa, despite being busy with Maddie and her mind reverted back to the affair. They had a get together with the family to give them the news of the pregnancy to everyone and as usual, Lawrence behaves as if he is so proud of the baby. He starts bragging on and on about how he stays up at night sometimes and feels really tired at work. My family has no idea that he stays up to chat with other women. No one knows that he doesn't help out at home at all. Yet, with the family around, he is running around, looking for glasses to serve drinks and he is sitting with everyone making jokes and entertaining everyone taking the limelight. Wow! Not seen him like this with his own growing family.

Lawrence asks Narissa's mum to help out, the very family he shunned once. Mum was very happy to help out when this new baby arrives, much to Narissa's relief.

The pregnancy felt short and Narissa got really busy with her daily chores. Max arrived in the early hours of the morning. It was an easier and quicker labour. As soon as Narissa thought her waters had broken, she told Lawrence. Lawrence called mum and dad at 5am. Narissa went into the hospital and Maddie stayed with grandparents. Maddie couldn't wait to see her sibling, still adamant that she is getting a brother.

While Narissa was pregnant with Max she had bought a book through a school fundraiser which was a beautiful book with pictures showing exactly how a baby is in a womb, the stages of growth, things a baby can do and the size of the foetus. Maddie told everyone all the time what the baby's size was when it was in the womb, in relation to her thumb or her hand. When she saw Max, she was really surprised, "where did the baby come from?" trying to lift the long top Narissa was wearing with the front opening buttoned up.

Maddie tried to look for cuts on Narissa's tummy and the Doctor who was taken by Maddie's curiosity, just told her frankly that the baby came from Mummy's vagina, which surprised Narissa. She couldn't say anything, after all the Doctor was the specialist.

By this stage Maddie is pushing herself around Narissa trying to find a comfortable place on the small hard hospital bed. "Mumma, does your vagina hurt?" She whispers.

"The head is really big!"

Narissa can almost see what Maddie is trying to get to here. How can a head this size fit through mum's vagina. We all just left it at that as Max was getting hungry. His soft lips, curly hair laced his forehead, fingers as soft as butter and pink hues of his skin made her heart just melt away. Narissa can recall Maddie in this position nearly 3 years ago. Pulling Maddie closer to herself she hugged her deep, feeling her comforting arms around herself. Why couldn't Lawrence hug her tenderly like this? She is longing for a hug from her husband who is unaware of any emotions and not thinking how he can comfort his wife at this stage.

'I don't know if I can love this child just as much as Maddie. I also don't want to neglect Maddie either.' Narissa was having some awful thoughts in her head, feeling divided, feeling sad for Maddie but excited for Max.

Narissa has even more work on her hands. Two children at different stages when Max is having a breast feed, Maddie needs her feed but she is getting very good feeding herself.

Double the trouble at home and Lawrence becomes even more self-absorbed. He won't be part of the children's lives at all. It is very hard to engage him in any family activities. Lawrence has never been able to discuss openly about any family affairs.

What surprises Narissa is that when they are out in the shopping centres or when they are around family he acts and behaves as if

She hung the clothes slowly in disappointment. Narissa saw Lawrence in the kitchen and came back into the house slowly. Before she could ask him anything, Lawrence came closer to her smiling with arms stretched out to give her a hug "would you like a cup of tea?"

"No, thank you!" She replied sternly.

"How could you? You left all the washing in the machine yesterday, you didn't hang them out, you didn't bring it back in and yet took all the praise for it when I was thanking you!" in a half tearful and half angry voice.

Narissa just brushed past Lawrence ignoring his affectionate gesture.

"Well darlin' I forgot." Lawrence says it casually.

"You forgot to do one little job I gave you and yet couldn't admit it? I don't understand you Lawrence. I don't know anyone who can do that. I have never met anyone who can be so deceiving. I mean you are just so childish and pathetic. I am finding it hard to believe." Narissa pulls out a dining chair and sits down.

"You could have been honest and told me that you forgot to put the washing on the line and didn't bring it in, instead of making yourself look good by lying." Narissa is sitting down feeling bemused.

"I don't get it. Truly, Lawrence, I don't understand this. I am your wife! I am not your mother!" Narissa can't help herself.

Lawrence just shrugged his shoulders and gave her a look that said 'well no big deal.' "What does it matter? It is on the line now?" Lawrence says casually. "I am making a cup of tea, would you like one?" he continues about the tea. Narissa knows he wants to make a cup of tea so he can sit down and read his paper for the rest of the day.

"You make so much fuss about little things." Lawrence goes about making two cups of tea. He can't seem to understand what Narissa's problem is.

"That's not little! You lied to me! You took false appreciation from me! Yet you didn't get up this morning to put the clothes on the line, fixing you-r mistake or actually telling me last night that you hadn't done any of it!" Narissa can't help herself and starts sobbing feeling really hurt inside.

It was winter and clothes get damp as the moisture sets in. The hassle of getting them in the dryer, plus Lawrence screaming about power bills which kept increasing due to Government tariffs was becoming too much to handle. Narissa was also studying a couple of papers at University to keep herself updated so she could keep her registration. 'I can't deal with this anymore!'

Narissa was a very career minded go getter type of girl before getting into this relationship. This kind of treatment from Lawrence was throwing her deeper into a weak soul and she was having melt downs more frequently. The changing hormones, lack of physical and emotional support was making her very emotional and tears would flow, without having time to think about anything. Sometimes Narissa didn't recognise her own self. She felt like she was someone else. The strong woman she used to be was just no more. She felt weak at all levels.

If she doesn't wash Lawrence's shirts one weekend, he would get wild. It has only happened once when Narissa was very tired and after doing several loads of sheets and towels and all tiddly baby clothes, she didn't manage to get Lawrence's shirts on the line, he growled at her on Monday morning because his favourite shirt was dirty and lying in the laundry basket. He would growl at Narissa like she was a little girl.

"Well, you could have remembered and done it yourself yesterday." She had replied feebly. Lawrence is always blaming Narissa for everything. She often forgave him in herself as she thought it was the stress of his work that was throwing him off balance. Everyone goes through life work stressful periods but the way Lawrence behaves, he makes it look like he is the only one suffering from stress and that he is extremely busy at work.

It seems like Narissa has to be the mother and the father in this family. She is the one who is the brain and the heart for the family.

Everything is lying on her shoulders and it is getting too much for her. She has had to get the ladder out to fix the garage door, put the pictures up, hang strings up to showcase her children's art work which Lawrence never paid any attention to. She is one who fixes the clothes line and then come inside to cook and read books.

Ella arrived with a quick, short labour. Again Maddie was right, she got her little sister. Max was just amazed at this tiny little baby and both Maddie and Max wouldn't leave Narissa alone. Max would sit as close as possible to Narissa, touching the baby's head as Narissa sat and breast fed, Maddie would sit and sing nursery rhymes or read a book.

Ella's name means light, beautiful, fairy, goddess and she truly suits this name. Again not chosen for the meaning but it suited the baby she was holding at the maternity ward a year ago. Ella loves to dress beautifully and always colour coordinated with glitter and sequins. She brings joy to my life even though she is quiet, reserved and dreamy, Ella would sing and sit with Narissa with a book and point out to pictures, clap and show so much love. The children gave Narissa so much joy that even if the sun didn't rise, the rays of sunshine in the house was enough to radiate the warmth for me.

Max's name means greatest, independence, leadership, and focus on large and important things. How did Narissa get this name? They just liked it, short and sweet.

Narissa tries to talk to Lawrence every day, filling him on all the happenings of the day and told him that she can understand his stress at work and finances but he needs to share more. Lawrence acts as though he is a really wealthy husband with a stay-at-home wife who takes care of him like a King and three children who he cares for, provides for and all out of love. Very proud of his achievements, but at the same time he brings Narissa down to tears at home with his put downs, inconsiderate comments, lack of involvement with everyday chores and running of the house. Narissa feels like she is on a yo-yo and it doesn't feel normal.

Narissa became a bit of a loner, absorbed in her children's world all on her own. The unknown world of child rearing, that is experimental and common sense. There wasn't any manual she could refer to. However, the library was a great source of information.

She found a book on "Talking to your children, so they listen" and another one on "How to listen so your children speak, 'Raising boys' and 'Raising Girls'.

Of course, sharing with Lawrence was not a good idea because he knew it all. He didn't need to learn anything at all. That was his attitude every time Narissa tried to read him some excerpts from the books.

Narissa decided to quit her job altogether because she had her hands full. Lawrence didn't want her working after the children arrived. 'Best way to keep myself sane was to get out and be active in the community.' She enrolled the children in the swimming lessons, play group, Gymbaroo, gymnastics and music. While taking them to all these activities, she made some really good friends as well. Most of the women were extremely caring, nice and chatty. It was great to share opinions, ideas, recipes and they were always looking for quick easy recipes for cakes, savouries and meals. Sometimes the women arranged play dates for the children and it was a great way to catch up for the mums as well who were running the household in isolation. They had a lot in common and therefore felt comfortable with each other discussing all the little incidences and their journey into motherhood.

One of the mum's at swimming lesson had a part time job at the local jewellery store. She wanted Narissa to job share with her. If Narissa could spare four hours a day for just two days a week was good for her employer. After thinking hard over a few weeks, Narissa decided to give it a go. Only obstacle to this was how does she approach Lawrence? He clearly doesn't want Narissa to have her own money, he had said several times, "Why do you need your own money? I work for all of us."

Narissa picked up some courage to approach Lawrence. "Honey, you know the little jewellery shop at the mall here, literally three minutes' drive from home, well, they want someone to come in for four hours per day for two days. I was thinking that I need to keep

but what a mistake. He won't have a bar of it. "Nah, there are better ones than this." was his lame reply.

With Lawrence, there is always something better out there especially if it is something he didn't think of or purchased. It took Narissa a long time to realise all this. She thought he was just a stubborn man.

Narissa didn't have her own computer so she couldn't use it but asked Lawrence if she could use his computer and put the program on. Instantly he shut her down. "I told you it is a useless program and someone has scammed you. Are you stupid? You want to ruin my computer?"

"Lawrence, everyone at the school uses it and they love it. Laura's husband is in IT and he recommended it. It can't be bad?" Narissa pleads with him. "I just want to try and see. It might make it easier to budget. There is no harm in trying something, is there?"

When Lawrence doesn't want to do something he walks away. He either gets quiet and ignores you or will argue till you feel helpless. It is best not to approach him because he will get angrier. It is his way or high way. So Narissa dropped it. He promised to find a better programme but that never happened. Instead he just decided to take over all the accounts and bill payments etc. Narissa was doing well except she thought this software she purchased for $10 might speed up the process and give her more time for other things, but not meant to be. Although, Lawrence taking over her job meant she was free of that duty, which was quite pleasing except she was worried about his lack of commitment to tasks.

After receiving several letters from the energy company, gas company and telephone company, big words in red saying 'overdue' and the letter went on to say "if you do not pay your bill by this particular date, your electricity supply will be terminated".

This happened several times over several months and Narissa was getting fed up of this. She approached Lawrence calmly and asked him what this was all about. She wanted an explanation. "We have never had this problem before" she said to him. Narissa had budgeted very well even without the Quicken program. It was obvious to her that Lawrence was not capable of managing funds and he took over because she was doing a good job.

'How could he do this to his family? Does he know the pain he causes me?' Narissa was trying to make sense.

That was the decider, he wouldn't manage the payments anymore!

She, once again took over the bill payments. Could she teach him how to manage time? Could she teach him about priorities in life? She could if he was willing to learn. Lawrence is a lazy man and likes to take easy way out of things. He likes to get into things when they are going well. But if things are not going well he will try to blame someone else and it was usually Narissa.

This whole arrangement didn't last very long either. The bank changed systems and Lawrence did the paper work for both and he set up the on-line banking and wouldn't disclose the password to Narissa or let her set up an internet banking. It meant she was kept in the dark. Lawrence now had full control of the banking and payments.

Lawrence was once sent on a time management course through work, which she thought was ridiculous at the time. Children learn time management at school, with everyday life skills and yet Lawrence being sent on a time management course meant there was something seriously wrong.

Lawrence had spent a whole day at this course and when he came home he raved on and on as if it he had learnt something new. In fact he wasn't telling Narissa anything new but she had to pretend that he went on a really useful course.

'Is this how life is supposed to be, so lonely at times, so full of pretence and fulfilling selfish desires and acting selflessly just to satisfy our own inner desires at someone else's expense?' Those days of showering each other with gifts of satin pyjamas, perfumes, flowers, kisses and chocolates, did it mean anything for the inner core of our feelings? Was it all an emulation of the sexual desires in ourselves that drove us to act in such precarious manner, regardless of what the future had in store?'

'My friend Becky used to say she won't get married because she hasn't found Mr Right yet. Is there a Mr Right anywhere? How do you know? So many books, advices but can you really smell a Narcissistic? Yes, well that's what I think I have married, a narcissistic man. How to recognise one is very difficult.'

'I wasn't promised anything when I was dating Lawrence, I thought he loved me. He loved everything about me. So can he suddenly have no interest in me?

The only thing that has changed is that I became a mother of three beautiful children. I adore my angels and feel that each one has a special gift. Should I be punished for this?'

*"When you truly love somebody, you will love them no matter how much torture they have put you through, because you can't imagine your world without them"* —*Mikhail Kriel*

# CHAPTER 3

*"A mother can feel a child even when they are physically apart."*

'MY HEAD IS buzzing with this little kid screaming continuously for three hours. My spine feels bruised, is aching continuously in places I cannot reach to inflict pain so I can relieve some pain. The muscles in my body feel numb from the stress. My eyes can barely stay open. When I lie on the soft pillow, a tear drops from my eye. I am not crying, my eye is just weepy. I feel numb all over. Even my heartbeat is so soft. I feel I have no pulse. So I check on my pulse. Thank goodness, I have a pulse. Somehow it feels like I am dead but not really dead. I can touch without any feeling, I can hold without any strength, I can see without knowing what I am seeing, I can hear without actually comprehending and I cannot sense anything around me. I don't know what happened, but everything is quiet. The silence of the night has put me into deep rest.

I have been nursing a baby all night. I must have dozed off a few times but it feels like I have been awake most of the night. I know all the noises of the night. The neighbours dogs that bark each time a sensor light goes on, the hustling noises of the trees and shrubs around us, the noise of the fridge and the heater that makes as the thermostat goes off and on.'

'I looked at my bedside clock, it's 3.30 am. I don't want to get out of bed. The atmosphere feels cold and it is pitch dark. The silence is unbearable. I slowly pull myself up and push myself out of the bed. I sat on the edge of the bed slowly lowering my feet to the cold ground. The normal soft wool carpet feels hard from the cold surroundings. I push myself up and now standing on my feet, I feel as though my back would break. The stiffness of my back makes me feel like I am an inflexible bit of wood. I think the epidural has had some effect on my spine. I had to have an epidural when I gave birth to Maddie. The long labour, the pain, the fear almost killed me and yet I have no regrets. Maddie is just so beautiful.'

Narissa takes each step cautiously and makes it to Maddie's room. She is resting. She shines the torch beside herself so that she doesn't wake Maddie up by shining it directly on her face. Maddie looks so peaceful. A quick check of her pulse satisfies Narissa and now can go back to bed and get some sleep.

3.40am and the baby monitor is showing some signs of movements. Narissa can hear the small noises coming through the monitor and went back to Maddie's room and it is all quiet. 'How odd? I am pretty sure I heard something.'

Narissa spent most of her night worrying, getting very little sleep and trying to keep her own ruffling in bed to a minimum. It will be mayhem for her if another child wakes up now.

There is no way that Lawrence will wake up. Nothing wakes him up, not even noises outside. The pets' meow, bark, kids cry, wind blows the trees, doors slam...nah nothing wakes Lawrence up.

In the morning Narissa woke up at a usual time of 6.30am. It was dark, quiet with a slight chill in the atmosphere. Winter is approaching. She needs to get the washing done, empty the dishwasher, prepare some breakfast. There are lunch boxes to be prepared, making sure there are some spare clothes in the bag, kids to pre-school and then go to work, may have to pop in to the grocery store as well.

When she married Lawrence they both took the marriage vows that said that they will be there for each other in sickness and in health. Narissa had thought that was what marriage was about. She had expected Lawrence to be part of her life in a way that families are, a lifelong companion, someone to hold your hand in bad times and laugh with you in good times.

It is now 7.00 am and Narissa is feeling exhausted. In fact she feels sick. 'I have a dry throat and feel really thirsty but I don't have a desire to drink. My head feels really heavy and I feel nauseous. I actually don't want to get out of bed because my body feels heavy, every bone feels heavy and tired. Do I have a choice? I do have choices, one is to stay in bed and say "I am sick" or I can just get up and take a Homeopathic remedy and rest or do I keep pushing myself.'

The last time Narissa was feeling this way was several months ago. She also had really heavy bleeding the day before. On that particular instance she actually made the choice of staying in bed. That's the day Lawrence shrieked at her and reminded her that he had to go to work and earn the money for the family. It wasn't his choice to raise children and so it wasn't his problem to take care of everything at home.

That particular day Narissa forced herself out of bed, tried to get the kids ready and off to school and then had to stop the car to vomit. She felt helpless and at the same time had to be strong for the children. She remembers crying but there were no tears.

Today, as she curls into the sofa, she melts like ice cube left on a hot concrete driveway. Her heart bleeds. Yes, that relationship that she called "love" was based on false hopes.

A narcissistic person is full of themselves. They see themselves as the most important being in the world. Lawrence couldn't take a day off or go in a bit late to work to help his family? His work was so important? He is allowed to take a day off to look after spouse or children but he doesn't take a day off. Not that Narissa is sick often. That day, that one day when she had said that she was too sick to take the kids to school, what did she get? A whole lot of abuse. She was made to feel like she was a weak woman, guilty for living off Lawrence's salary and a total loser. Narissa had worked before and had money saved up and also wanted to get into property investments so that she won't have to ask him for money when they had children. She had no idea that she will ever get into this situation.

'I see Lawrence taking off to work, straight after his breakfast leaving all his dishes on the kitchen bench hurriedly disappearing down the stairs. Did he offer any help? Nope!'

Despite knowing he has a sick wife and there are children to be taken care of, Lawrence takes off as if he doesn't live there. In his neatly ironed shirt, sleek freshly dry cleaned suit, polished shoes and hair brushed with hair products that only girls would dream of applying, Lawrence disappears from sight. He didn't even look back to see Narissa at the doorway upstairs. How could he be so reckless? How could he be so insensitive and uncaring? Narissa was getting more livid with herself because no matter what she did she was the loser.

Who do you talk to when things like this strike you? Go to a Doctor and they might say you have baby blues, but Narissa doesn't hurt her children loves them dearly. She does a lot of things together and spends a lot of time with them. She read about baby blues syndrome and it didn't fit the picture. She only get angry sometimes but that's mostly when she has physical aches and pain. She feels emotionally vulnerable. If she talks to family or friends they don't get the full picture. They are not feeling her pain. They say, "have a cup of tea, sit down and breathe; take a break; leave house work for another day." Narissa does those things anyway. She just needs someone to hug her and just tell her that she is doing a great job. Someone to just hold her and tell her that they are there for her. Someone to tell her that it is ok to lie down and have a nap. It will be nice if Lawrence could just sometimes be part of her life emotionally.

'Do people think you don't know these petty advices? The Doctor might send me to a Psychologist and I will need several appointments for which I don't have the funds for. Plus they will try to teach me to deal with the way I feel. Now I will be more twisted. Although it will help me to cope with life, it will not 'fix' what I am feeling. I think my dis-ease will get deeper inside my body.' Narissa is analysing it hard.

'I don't have any injuries so Physiotherapy is out of question. What about massage. Yes, I could. How do I pay for it? Who will look after the children?

I don't have time nor money to go for a massage. I can't call upon a friend because I have called upon a friend to help once and Lawrence made me feel bad. He thought I was trying to make him look like he was a selfish man, even though the truth is not far from it.'

Besides, Lawrence complained about money all the time. He accused Narissa of not understanding the expanses as if she was dumb. Narissa had saved up money and also talked about investments and talked about life after children and how they were going to survive on one income. Lawrence didn't pay any attention?

In fact it wasn't easy to have a discussion with Lawrence. He somehow managed to put Narissa down, turn every discussion into an argument and there was never a closure on anything. Narissa was always left in a limbo and couldn't make big decisions herself because she didn't have the support. Sometimes she just needed a sound board, someone to listen to her opinions and ideas and someone to give her a bit of assurance.

One of Narissa's friends invited herself for a coffee on a Friday morning except on the actual day Narissa was just not up to it. Felicity called and Narissa decided to take a rain check but Felicity wasn't one for giving up easy. She insisted on going over. Narissa gave in as she thought she could do with some company anyway and Felicity would give her a hand with chores as she was one of those who will come to your place and put the kettle on without asking. This is something Narissa really liked in Felicity as she was just so helpful. Her husband had a share in the company he worked for and he travelled a lot through his work. They had a lovely relationship. After 10 years of marriage he seemed to still love her a lot. If he was away for a week, he always made sure

Felicity had time away from the children. She might go shopping to Melbourne or they would have a family vacation in Fiji. He would buy her expensive diamond rings or bracelets for mother's day or her birthday, which he always remembered. When Felicity came in she was horrified. "You look awful! Look at ya! All pale and like a dead soul. C'mon, give me a hug." Felicity comes running to Narissa with open arms and glazed eyes.

'I hadn't seen myself in the mirror so I had no idea what I looked like'. "I feel ok." I replied.

"You are not! By the way, where is Lawrence? Surely, he didn't leave you in this way!" Felicity is walking around the house as if to find Lawrence hiding behind a sofa or a door.

"He has gone to work. You know he has a mountain of work." I am trying to justify his absence. This is normal me now. I am always justifying Lawrence's lack of involvement with the family.'

"Anyway, sit down. I need to make us a cuppa and then we can decide what to do. Perhaps you call Lawrence and let him know that you are very unwell. Let me talk to him as well." Felicity is not happy. 'I can tell by the urgency in her voice.'

"Hey, I will be fine. Truly. I just need some rest. Lawrence is very busy as you know and pulling him home will not do any of us any good." Narissa puts on a brave face trying to calm Felicity. Narissa has become good at this. She can put on different masks herself now.

After a cuppa, Felicity put all the washing out and then she fed the children and cleaned the floor. She made Narissa some lunch and then left because she had a pedicure appointment which she couldn't cancel. Felicity and Sean were on their way to a romantic weekend away while Sean's parents looked after the children. Felicity has 3 boys and it is a handful. At least she gets time away. Felicity wanted to cancel her weekend away and help Narissa out but she won't let Felicity do that. Sean's unpredicted work travel requirements meant they had to do see their plan through because you just don't know when they will be able to get away again. "No Filli, you go ahead and have a fabulous weekend." Narissa insisted.

Felicity made Narissa promise that she will ask Lawrence for help when he comes home. Narissa knows that she can't. Everything she says falls on deaf ears.

When Lawrence finally arrived home after 9pm, Narissa was already half dead. "Oh what's with you? You don't even work as hard as me." Lawrence comments as he lays his condescending eyes on Narissa.

'I didn't know whether to scream, cry or ignore him. I wanted to wring his neck. I took some deep breaths and told him that my friend Felicity had popped over this morning. I mentioned that I was unwell and Felicity came around as she was anyway, but she gave me a hand with some chores around the house.'

"So I see, you can have coffee mornings while I slave away." Lawrence replied with sarcasm in his voice and eye brows raised as if reprimanding a young kid.

"Let me finish before you judge." I am giving myself space between words so that I don't exhaust myself out.

"Felicity came over to catch up. I need some adult company too. But I have been feeling really low and kind of sick. Felicity was going to call and ask you to come home to give me a hand today." I looked at Lawrence while saying all this and I could see he was getting agitated.

"Why? What does she know about my work? Didn't you tell her how busy I am?" Lawrence screams out.

"Stop yelling. I don't want the kids to wake up, please. I am exhausted." I feel like I will break down.

"Well you brought this upon yourself. And now you have made me look like an inadequate husband." Lawrence is shuffling his suit on the coat hangers in the wardrobe.

Narissa didn't have the energy to fight him so she just told him to have his dinner as she was too tired to eat.

Narissa woke up the next morning feeling a bit rested and went to the kitchen. She was so disappointed to see all the pots and pans on the ceramic stove top and plate's half sitting in the deep kitchen sink. Her heart sank. Lawrence didn't eat but he didn't clean up either. She looked outside the window and his car had gone. He had already left home.

It was a Saturday morning so Narissa didn't have to rush out the door and often took it easy. She had all the pots to empty out and wash them. The rice had hardened in the cooker which needed soaking and the casserole dish was the same. Dishwasher loaded up, kids fed and slowly dragging the laundry basket to get clothes in the washing machine, she felt weak as. She heard Lawrence's car in the driveway. He walked into the house full of beans, whistling and singing with the paper in one hand and a plastic bag which looked like from Bunnings hardware store, ready to do some work. When Lawrence is happy, the whole world is expected to be happy.

"You didn't eat last night?" Narissa asked Lawrence.

"Nah, we went out. Remember, it was Friday night. The boys went for drinks so we decided to eat." Lawrence replies. He 'talks as if I am no one to him'.

"Wow, Lawrence. You had to go to work on Friday because you wanted to go out for dinner with the boys. You could have told me."

'Right now I am crying inside. How could someone be so cruel? He didn't eat but surely he knew I was tired, I am sure he could see that. He could have cleaned up for me", thought Narissa.

"I didn't eat and it wasn't my dishes to clean." Lawrence told me carelessly. He is so uncaring.

"You could have cleaned up!" I exclaimed.

"Well, it is Saturday and you are home. So what's the big deal? You can do it now." Lawrence tells.

"Who the fuck am I, Lawrence? Am I your slave? Is this what your mother taught you?" I can't help myself. I feel like having a real fight with him but he doesn't care and that makes me want to fight him more.

"You are so childish!" Lawrence looks at me with eyes like a hawk.

"How am I childish? Don't you think of giving a helping hand to someone at all? Oh sorry, I forgot, you only help people outside of home." Narissa said it quickly and left.

'Today I want to smack him, I want to spit on him, I want to pull his hair out and I want him to feel the pain.'

'Unfortunately, I am not capable of such acts. I swallow my grief, my desires and damage my soul just because Lawrence is the father of my children and because I loved him for who he was when I met him.

I felt selfish and really grose inside for having such feelings for him right now. How could I be made to feel like this? I am not this kind of person but what have I become? Is there any other woman in this world who feels this way?'

Narissa's thoughts wondered off to all her friends from different groups and they have a very different experience with their husbands. They always share their experiences and Narissa can never compare so she keeps quiet. Most women's husbands cook on a Saturday, bring home flowers, and wash up after dinner, read books to the children. One of the ladies from the Gymbaroo group told the group how her husband does all the baking in the house. Most men cooked one day a week even though most of the mums in the groups stayed home.

'Then why have a landed myself a lemon?' thought Narissa.

'I read somewhere once that God doesn't give you something you can't handle. Why does God think that I can handle all of this? I feel I need help of some sort but I am losing faith in God.'

'I should have studied Psychology because the human mind just intrigues me' thought Narissa. She studied a couple of Psychology units at University but found it very boring. Falling asleep in lectures when the lecturer was going on and on about Jung's theory or Freudian theories made Narissa realise that she was more of a hands on learner rather than a reading about other people's theories. While trying to read a book by Carl Jung she couldn't get past the first page. She somehow managed to scrape through the Psych unit and passed with just 52%. No big deal, a pass was a pass.

Researching and learning was her favourite pass time. She was gravitating more and more towards the self-healing type of books, mind body connections and it was fascinating, learning to differentiate between different mental illnesses was quite interesting. Narissa didn't like giving labels, but she knew that the different personality types existed and it was important to differentiate and deal with people differently.

A few of the kids at the pre-school were diagnosed with Asperger's syndrome, ADHD and were on medications. The mothers were extremely exhausted all the time. They got extra help from their husbands and families, which was important because Narissa could only imagine how difficult their lives would have been. Having 3 children of her own and under 5 years of age at one stage was exhausting in itself, but to raise children diagnosed with some mental disorder was unimaginable.

Narissa wondered if Lawrence was suffering from something. It wasn't easy talking to him about anything. He just gets totally defensive and abusive if you ever tried to talk to him about anything. Lawrence always felt that Narissa was attacking him. Narissa thought she had 'normal' children with normal kids needs and she just had to figure out ways to deal with every stage in their lives. According to Lawrence their children were too demanding and attention seekers.

"Well, look at them. They are racing off everywhere in the zoo as if the whole place is theirs. They can't sit in one place and eat like normal children."

I look at Lawrence in awe. What the hell is he going on about?

"Look at Ella, chasing butterflies and not thinking where she is going."

"When I was little I wasn't allowed to do anything. I never visited a zoo. I wasn't allowed to play with friends." Lawrence looks into thin air.

Lawrence told me once at the zoo that he thought the children were spoilt and too demanding.

"Why do you say that?" I asked looking at him and really trying to understand him.

"Lawrence, they are just being kids. That's what children do. Run around chasing butterflies, rainbows, not thinking where they are going. Children don't really care." I explained to him.

"But they are so selfish!" "What if they get hurt?" Laurence is getting angry.

"Honey, listen. So what if they fall chasing a butterfly?" I asked.

"They will fall, maybe get a little graze and they will learn. No big deal." Narissa said with a sly smile, remembering her own childhood.

'I used to play outside a lot. I used to talk to the plants and feel the fresh wind brush my face with travelling fragrances of flowers and pine trees. It really uplifted me and I felt so free.'

She watched her girls running around freely, clapping hands and smiles that make you want to run and join them. The beautiful manicured green lawns at the zoo was the perfect place for the girls to run around freely. Her girls were really enjoying themselves. The little giggles and occasional burst of laughter made Narissa really proud of their happiness.

Lawrence really had a problem with children running around, feeling free and enjoying themselves. He was always speculating someone getting hurt, sometimes coming across as a real paranoia.

Lawrence didn't like it when kids fell and got messy. He didn't like the extra care he had to give. He always wanted kids to be incident free and that meant he expected Narissa to run after the children when they were playing.

Maddie would have been 4 when they had gone for a long walk. It was a really pleasant afternoon and Narissa managed to get Lawrence to come out to the park.

She realised that he came with them because he wanted to find out about the park where he was going to play a game of cricket with his work colleagues. Lawrence needs to know beforehand how to get to some place and where to go. He wanted to see the pitch because he wants to outsmart everyone. Therefore, coming out to the park was for his own benefit. It didn't matter to Narissa because it meant that at least he was there with the family.

Pushing the pram with Max in it, Ella in the back pack and Maddie walking and skipping alongside Narissa, singing nursery rhymes on a beautiful Sunday afternoon, with the sun shining behind them as it was slowly moving west with still some warmth left in its rays, everything was going well. Apart from Maddie singing, Max pointing to the cars that travelled fast past them and Ella just breathing the fresh air and pointing to the beautiful butterflies that flew past, Narissa and Lawrence were walking in silence. Suddenly Maddie tripped and fell on her knees. Maddie had blood pouring down her left knee and started screaming, obviously hurting from the fall which made her land right on her knee. Lawrence screamed at her for tripping and then held her arms pushing her to get up and walk home. I could see Maddie really uncomfortable and in a lot of pain. According to Lawrence, she had to toughen up but he couldn't see how she was unable to put her foot on the ground and walk even in a hobble.

"Daddy, it hurts." Maddie cries out. "Daddy, it really hurts." Maddie is usually tough but the way she sat on the ground and the look on her face showed that it must have been really painful. She must have landed on her knee cap and the amount of blood pouring was enough to make anyone sick.

Lawrence is still telling Maddie off for falling and asking her to get up and toughen up.

Narissa quickly put the brakes on the pram and managed to get a towel which she carries in the pocket of the pram with water and snacks. She held the towel firmly on the graze. With Ella in the back pack it was a little bit difficult to get down fully so she looked up at Lawrence for some help.

"Lawrence, perhaps you could give me a hand. I think Maddie will have to be carried." Narissa looks up to talk to Lawrence who doesn't seem to want to know anyone at this point.

Narissa had Maddie on one hip and Ella on her back pack and unable to move, she looked at Lawrence to push the pram. It was awkward and really uncomfortable but Narissa kept telling herself that home was a few meters away when in fact it was half a kilometre away or probably more. Narissa pushed the pram awkwardly for a bit and Lawrence reluctantly took over. He basically pushed Narissa to a side and started pushing the pram. Narissa struggled to keep Maddie on her hips as her right knee now wrapped in a towel with blood soaking through had to be kept away from banging into anything. The frame of the back pack was cutting into Narissa's back as well but she had no choice but to continue walking down the street.

As soon as they turned the corner Narissa could see the house, she felt a sigh of relief. "Not long to go now" she says in a hopeful voice, hoping Maddie will feel relieved even though Narissa knew there was good 15-20 meters left. They arrived home with a bit of effort, Narissa feeling exhausted and sore herself from carrying Maddie on her hips and Ella on the back pack with a frame that kept bouncing on her back.

Lawrence just disappeared. He left Max in the pram and walked off.

"Lawrence! Lawrence, can you take Max while I take care of Maddie, please?" Narissa is pleading.

"Just going to the toilet." replies Lawrence.

Putting Maddie down gently on the sofa in the family area, Narissa assured Maddie that it will get better.

"I am sorry, mumma. I am really sorry." Maddie is trying to make eye contact with Narissa. "Mumma, I don't know how I fell."

"Don't worry about that, Maddie. Accidents happen. We will get this cleaned and wash with Dettol and then you can just rest. It will be alright, you understand." Narissa assures Maddie.

Now Narissa has to get the buckles off and lower Ella' back pack, get her out and then get Max who is sitting in the pram in the garage. Lawrence is still in the toilet.

Ella is out and Max is in the house. They must be hungry and thirsty now as well.

Narissa got a basin of cold water bath and nursed Maddie's knee, applied some calendula and bandaged it. The bleeding seemed to have settled down now but the white of the knee cap was showing and the wound was bigger than originally thought. Since there was no skin left on the knee cap, Maddie was feeling the pain.

"Mumma, daddy is angry with me. But Mumma, I didn't fall on purpose." Maddie is trying to hold Narissa's face with both her hands and tell her right in her face.

"We know you didn't fall on purpose, Maddie. Daddy is not angry, ok." Narissa has to keep reassuring Maddie.

One dose of Arnica pillules and Maddie should be good.

Lawrence came out of the toilet just as Narissa had sat the kids at the small table with sliced up apples dowsed with some yoghurt.

"Can't take these kids anywhere without any incidences. Why did she have to fall like that?" Lawrence walks in shouting.

"No one does this on purpose!" Narissa had to shout back at Lawrence.

It seemed that Lawrence thought Maddie could have avoided the fall or somehow Narissa who was already pushing the pram and had the back pack on her, should have somehow been supervising her. He couldn't accept the fact that these things happen and that we just need to deal with little accidents like this.

'When I think about these little incidences I realise that Lawrence has a real issue with helping anyone in need especially his own family. In fact he thinks people can somehow avoid incidences and if they can't then don't do it when he is around. He is just not capable of showing empathy, remorse or sadness for anyone in the family.'

What really baffles Narissa is that Lawrence shows a lot of empathy when out of home and usually when there are a lot of people around. He will go and help little kids in need and help other mum's with opening doors and lifting prams for them, but not for Narissa. 'Is he a misogynist?' Narissa can't stop thinking about this.

Poor Maddie ended up with an infection in her knee, a few weeks later and the Doctors had said just to bathe with warm water, Dettol and keep it open for it to heal. The knee was a difficult place and to teach a 4 year old to keep the knee straight at all times was not easy. Every night became a ritual of changing bandages so Maddie could get to sleep. For pre-school Maddie had to have a plaster over so that dirt won't get into the sore. In all this time Lawrence never offered once to help out with Max and Ella or any of the household chores.

'I didn't think too much of it at that time as I just got on with my everyday chores and focussed totally on the children, the house and my studies.'

"The greatest act of loving another person is letting go and wishing for their happiness and well-being regardless of your sorrow and pain" —*Anurag Prakash*

# CHAPTER 4

*Positive energy can bring strength and motivation*

I T IS 7.30AM and the sun is shining bright as a search light and the sky is unbelievably blue with just a few speckles of white clouds around. Narissa is in a good mood because it is a bright day.

She tries not to let the gloomy days overtake her emotions. She always bounce back quickly, in fact she has no choice, with three beautiful children who remind her every day that life is worth living.

Some mornings the kids watch Barney and some days it is Humphrey bear. In the afternoon they might watch a bit of Thomas the Tank Engine or maybe Pingu. All these programmes are short and that's really good for the children because their attention span is short. Narissa adored her and working at the local primary school she thought she will make a lot of difference to the children in this world. She cared for them like her own. Teaching in classroom was not just the book learning. They discussed life skills and enjoyed baking with them, singing with them, playing with playdough, building castles with bricks and bobs.

Narissa's patience has been really tested since her three angels arrived into this world. She has learnt to be calm, collected and patient with any situation, even when they are faced with uncertainties.

She clearly remembers this incident as if it just happened yesterday. Narissa had filled the baby bath, ran to the room to get the baby and came back to find Max sitting in the baby bath with diaper on. She had to run back to the bedroom and get Ella back into her cot, rescue Max and the quick thinking solved the problem by running a bath for Max and then getting his diaper off which had like fifty litres of water, almost half the baby bath tub water, go back and get Ella. Phew!

One of her friends called that afternoon just as Narissa just sat down. "Angela! Hi"

Angela was one of the mum's at pre-school and Maddie used to love going to her house for play dates with Claire who was in the same group activities with Maddie. Angela had called to see if she could pick Maddie from pre-school and take her home with her. She was just so thoughtful and all Narissa had to do was inform the pre-school that Maddie was going on a play date. Angela thought it was easier for Narissa to just stay home with the other two children instead of picking Maddie from pre-school with other two children tagging along, dropping her off, then going back home and coming back to Angela's to pick Maddie up.

"Your timing couldn't be perfect, Angela. I have had such a poo of a morning." Narissa went on to describe her day and Angela immediately responded, "Hey Narissa listen, just make yourself a cuppa and put your feet up. Don't do anything else. Promise? You need a break. I will get Maddie and call you so you can talk to her and I will bring her back home later around 5? You need to pamper yourself. Get Lawrence to give you a massage tonight." She giggles.

'If only I can get Lawrence to do anything.' Narissa thought with a sigh. Lawrence is no use in the evenings. Usually he works late, comes home, gobbles his dinner and sits in front of the TV with his computer on his lap and keeps complaining about how much work he has and how behind he is in his work. No idea why he is always behind when he starts early, finishes late and works in front of the TV. Acts like he is the only man on earth that works. Narissa doesn't work according to Lawrence. He never even asks her what sort of a day she had had. She always asks him how his day had been.

Narissa wanted to stay at home for her children as she didn't like the childcare centres. She had visited a few but decided that the children will be better off at home in a caring nurturing environment plus she didn't want to miss any of their milestones. Lawrence didn't like the idea of paying the child care centre for his kids anyway. She tried to discuss with Lawrence but he refused to be part of any discussion and Narissa left on her own had to basically cope on her own.

Narissa thought that when the kids were off breastfeeding she could get a part-time job or work at nights when Lawrence was home, but that didn't happen. She told Lawrence that she had found a job at a Laboratory doing culture work. You only needed basic science knowledge which Narissa had as she had studied some science papers at university so she was going to start work at 7pm and finish at 10.00pm for 3 nights a week.

She accepted the job but on her first day of work, Lawrence didn't come home till 6.45pm. She told the kids that she will be out at work and they had to be really good for dad. They had all cooperated, showered, had dinner and were in bed after reading their books.

"Mumma, will you be late?" Maddie is always so concerned.

Narissa brought it up with Lawrence the next day but he just shrugged his shoulders and ignored her. She got really mad with him, "Lawrence, it is not fair that I have a job and I am late every day. Can you please make an effort and be home by 6.30 at least on the three days that I have to work? I don't make you late for your work?"

"Who asked you to go to work? Plus, my job pays for everything around here." He just bragged.

'Wow! I hadn't expected that, such arrogance. What does he think, that I am not capable of earning and yet he was boasting to everyone before getting married that his wife was a university graduate and planning on doing a Ph.D., which turned out to be just a show off thing to his family and friends?'

"What do you get paid? Is it that important that you have to go to work at night?" Lawrence shrieks out without even looking at Narissa.

"Excuse me! You are the one who tells me to go fetch my own money to buy clothes, shoes and coffees. You don't want to pay me and yet you don't want me to work either. Are you stupid?" Narissa is shouting angrily.

Narissa was late for work and sheepishly walked into the lab. The other ladies were all there at their stations and she apologised to them. Narissa made an excuse, "sick kids, you know what's it like."

This scenario repeated on several occasions. Lawrence wouldn't come home on time. Narissa had to call the laboratory and make excuses. She had run out of all the excuses, sick kids, car won't start, mother called, Husband late and what else.

One day her boss shouted at her. "You have a sick kid almost every week and you are late! Can you explain this?"

"You have made mistakes in your work and last night you left the incubator door ajar! Do you realise the damage this causes to our work? Its kids or something else! Is there anything else left?"

Narissa just melted down. She went to the office and told her boss that it was better for her to finish off at the end of the week because her husband can't get home on time to look after the children. She also mentioned that it was very difficult for her to fund a baby sitter at this stage and it was better that she just left work completely.

Regrettably she handed in her resignation. He boss didn't say anything and neither did the rest of the staff. They could all see that it was in the best interest for Narissa to focus on her family. There was no leaving party nor cards or flowers. That was the end of her working.

Weird part is that Lawrence started staying at work till nine and even later sometimes, not that he earned any more than he used to. He never bothered asking Narissa what had happened to her part time work and never bothered asking how she was coping with everything.

Narissa didn't realise how and when she slipped into this mode of being scared to be "me". How she became a part of somebody else's desires how she became so submissive and lost her independence. 'I don't know when I became who I am today. I am not sure how to describe myself. I am a mother and yet I feel inadequate and yet I sometimes feel I am a damn good one but my husband doesn't think so!'

Narissa accepted the fact that she was going to enjoy every bit of being at home with her children and absorb herself with fun activities. Her days were very well planned and organised. She watched a bit of TV in the morning with the children learning colours, alphabets and numbers. Then they pack up and go to pre-school. Packing into her day included swimming lessons, Gymbaroo, dancing, going to the local parks or play dates and it is a total fun time.

By the end of the day though, Narissa was exhausted. Sometimes she just wanted to sleep. Her body was craving for a hug from someone, anyone. 'It will be so nice just to be reminded that I have done a wonderful job today. Someone who will just remind me that I am still a wonderful person and have some value in life. Someone to remind me that I am a human being and it is all going to be ok.'

'I really want to do something as I feel my brain is overloaded with children's things. I need to have some adult time.' She thought to herself.

Lawrence provides no company when he comes home. He rants about his work, gulps his dinner and then off he disappears. He never listens to what Narissa has to say, he never asks her anything about her day or the children even when she tells him the milestones. She shows him the children's art work and he just makes fun of them. Narissa realised that he was just not interested in anything or anyone.

Narissa being a good planner always had everything worked out in her head. Every single hour, minute or second she spends thinking, re thinking, planning her day, not just for today but for tomorrow, the day after and the rest of the week. When children have a sleep in the afternoon she tries to squeeze in some studies. Narissa was studying this business course to help her get a job when children are older.

'Thinking of my assignments sends me shivers. How am I going to get them done? I don't have a computer. I have to hand write everything. I asked Lawrence for a computer and he said he will get one since he has more knowledge in this field. Well two years later I am still waiting. Each time I bring it up, he tells me that he hasn't got any money or has been really busy at work.' He tells her off and it was getting harder and harder to talk to him.

Busy at work or an excuse, like a cover up for forgetting. Years later Narissa discovered that he didn't want her to have a computer, reason being? The internet is a dangerous medium. Narissa could meet someone and run away with them, just like one of Lawrence's mate's wife did. She was a high school graduate with no other tertiary education and stayed home with no interests or hobbies while hubby worked all day. The wife met someone on the internet and left off with them. But we can't blame the internet, although Lawrence thinks he can protect Narissa from everything.

'I wish I could go out and get a computer myself. I hate going into the city. The hustle and bustle of the cars, slow moving buses that block your view from where you want to get to, people jay walking everywhere, all these people with nice clothes on and shoes that I can't afford. The eating places make me so hungry. The smell of beautiful coffee from Starbucks that seems to be in every corner, the deep fried smells from MacDonald's and cake shops...yummm. The velvety icing on the cup cakes are not just good to look at but a small bit on the tip of my tongue sends me to ecstasy. Honestly I could get an orgasm just by licking the icing especially when it is chocolate.'

'Nah, can't do it. I am never on my own.' thought Narissa.

One day she picked up the courage to go into town with all three children in tow. It means getting the pram, unfolding it while kids sit impatiently in the car trying to pull the seat belt off. Narissa was talking not to anyone in particular but to herself because the kids were not listening. She finally get the pram out, remembering to get the toys in, get one child out. Oops wrong one, Max goes to the front so she should get the back one in first, meaning Ella. It seems like half hour has gone by and Narissa was still fiddling with the kids. People have walked past her in droves and she was sure some have come back the same path and seen her struggling. Max in, Ella in and Maddie wants to push the pram. Today's outing is to a small bookshop.

'Yes we are mobile now. We are moving at a snail pace. Shoot! There's a toy shop and let me push the pram a bit faster so the children cannot see the toy shop. Okay, I am mad thinking that they don't know the Toy world sign.'

It is a bright yellow sign and the words are in primary colours. The kids cannot miss the sign.

First stop is at Toy World. As soon as they got to the entrance, "mumma, I need to pee" Maddie tells Narissa in a sweetest voice. Great! The good thing is this city is wonderful because it is well catered for kids.

'I ask the shop assistant to show us the bathrooms. Can't push the whole pram in so I park the pram outside the door. I can still see the little ones while Maddie goes to bathroom. Now I need to go too. No I will hold on as it is not safe to leave children unattended in a pram with a 4 year old supervising.' Narissa is folding her legs so her desire to pee stops.

Finally out of the bathroom and now kids want to buy some toys. Narissa's cunning plan had worked in the past. She had got them to play with the toys then say 'goodbye' to the toys and then make a real quick exit.

It is not working today. Max is 2 and decides to play stubborn today. He wants this toy. The price is not in Narissa's reach and she tries to convince him that he can buy a better one. That in her term means a cheaper toy. It ain't working. He is now having a tantrum. He is pulling his hair, screaming, stomping his feet, every now and then gives an awful screech.

Looks like Ella needs a feed. Narissa thought it might be a good idea to get them to play a bit more while she feeds Ella. Gosh breastfeeding is so easy. It is like having your feed on tap. Narissa is very lucky that she never had any problems with breastfeeding. In fact she had endless supply of milk and her children always latched on to the nipple very well. Too well that sometimes they won't let go. Maddie had tried to chew on the nipple when she was breastfeeding and that had hurt a lot.

Narissa tries to sit, feeling her full bladder squeezing down her pelvis and pushing down her vagina. As it happens after 3 natural births, the vaginal opening is very open, the elasticity has gone like a well dried strip of your underwear where there is no more elasticity left. So while she is feeding, Narissa squeezes in some pelvic floor exercises.

Haven't quite finished and Maddie is hungry. That's ok because Narissa always brings crackers, cheese, dried fruits, nuts, fresh fruit and pots of yoghurt with her.

Max has stopped his tantrum and is playing with trucks, while Maddie decides to have a few crackers and needs to have a fluffy now.

Almost done, they walk out of the shop as quickly as possible without buying anything and Narissa is feeling rather good about herself. Just before the bookshop is a tiny little cafe.

"Mumma! Fluffy!" Maddie stands still pointing to the cafe.

'So at least I get to have a coffee.' Thought Narissa. After placing the order at the counter, Narissa walks over to the table where she has placed the pram with Maddie sitting at the table. Narissa had to go back and get her order. She got the fluffy for Maddie and Max, a bowl of chips, sandwiches and sat down. Kids are happy but she realised that she forgot to order her coffee. She couldn't be bothered going back to order. She watched the waitress serving others and it looked like the coffee was taking a long time to make, plus the place smells of workers from the office who have been in air-conditioned offices. The food place is nothing fancy and Narissa is not sure how clean everything is. Maybe if someone came and offered to order her coffee, she might be inclined to say 'yes'.

An hour later, they are all off to the book store and at this stage, Narissa needed to pee. 'I am sure I have leaked a bit in my pants and before the vagina opens up to let out all of it I must get to a bathroom. How on earth am I going to keep the children safe while

I am eliminating my waste? I asked the cafe if they could mind the children for me while I took a leak.'

Thank goodness we live in a world where we can still trust people. What a risk though! Thought Narissa.

Finally they arrived at the book store and it is now 1pm. Ella needs her sleep, Max might sleep and as for Maddie, who knows. At this stage Narissa doesn't plan to stay for long at the book store. After quick browsing through some books, she made a quick purchase of some colouring books and found some amazing story books for the kids and Walla! All done!

Getting back into the car, same things in reverse order. Maddie tries to help Narissa with unpacking the pram, then she got Ella in, Max in, Maddie in and now trying to fold the pram down so she can get it into the car. Do you think it will fold down? This stupid thing, which Narissa is now vigorously trying to push down won't unleash.

Unable to get the pram to fold down, Narissa opened the boot and chucked the whole thing in the car. Lucky for the big 7 seater Prado, she was able to put it in as is, without unfolding.

On the way home, 2 children are sleeping. Maddie is probably tired from all that walking and the noise of the city. The dust, the noise pollution and people overdose has probably made her head spin.

If Maddie sleeps in the car now she will be up all night. The Plunket nurses always reminded everyone to be very regimental with all these habits. Narissa was trying to talk to her and sing with Maddie so she stayed up.

Arriving home Narissa felt exhausted herself. She had to unpack and transfer each child to their respective beds. Maddie darling is holding off. So they sat down on the comfortable low sofa and looked through the purchases and then left Maddie alone with the books. Narissa feels like a rest herself but instead decides to bring the washing in. She has to start preparing dinner now in case the children wake up and she gets tied up. The phone goes off, but sorry no time. Narissa gulped a glass of water to quench her thirst from the overdose of pollutants today.

Getting back into the lounge she finds little darling Maddie fast asleep. Now Narissa feels totally guilty. She hasn't had a feed and has fallen asleep in her dirty clothes. She made her comfortable on the sofa, kissed her soft cheeks and forehead. Her hair smells of dust and sweat and her fingers feel sticky. 'Oh Maddie, she is a very special child.' Narissa whispers to herself.

As soon as Narissa gets up from her kneeling position next to Maddie on the sofa, she hears the baby monitor making noises. There is someone on the line. Sounds like Ella is up and needs a feed. So she ran upstairs, and in a few minutes was feeding Ella in the most uncomfortable position sitting on the edge of the bed, knowing very well that this is not a good thing. Now Max is up too. Narissa tries to hold him as well and starts to sing nursery rhymes but it looks like that he is hungry too.

The baby in her arms, latched onto her nipples which are feeling tender as the soft lips are trying to pull it in place while Narissa walks downstairs holding Max's fingers. He is very sweaty too.

They all made it downstairs, leaving Ella in the day cot and getting a drink of water for Max. Max is hungry. He is rubbing his tummy and feeling aggressive from hunger. Narissa dished his dinner with speed while Ella is screaming. She was told that pacifiers are not to be used as a comfort device and also told that they damage the shape of children's gums and teeth. So Narissa doesn't own one and has to put up with the screaming. She is used to all the screaming, crying, cooing and singing.

She rushed over, picked up Ella again and latched her to the nipple while feeding Max. He's happy to feed by himself but sometimes needs a bit of guidance. It is now 5.45pm.

Phew! Another day passing by and Narissa is feeling as if she has not achieved anything. All the feeding over, tidying up over, dishes in the dishwasher and she settles down on the floor cushions, which she made herself and felt very proud of, trying to play with the children. Going through the books they bought today was really fun.

It is bath and sleep time but Maddie hasn't woken up yet. The bath is upstairs and Narissa is going to get started. Narissa ran upstairs to run the bath and get Max in the big bath with small amount of water so if he fell in he won't drown. Ella is in the small bath. They hurried through the bath ritual today because Narissa was conscious about the fact that Maddie was sleeping on the sofa by herself. She must be extremely exhausted, otherwise she would have woken up by now.

We love bedtime because that's when Narissa gets the time to lie down, put her feet up, rest her head and snooze a bit. Everyday can be a different story though. Today, Narissa is not enjoying herself because she feels divided, not just emotionally but at some physical level she is feeling uncomfortable.

Ella is lying in her cot and playing with her baby mobile (colourful toys with music), Max is in his bed with a book on dinosaurs.

In the meantime Maddie has woken and she is terrified. It has suddenly gone dark and she can't see anyone. The curtains are open and she can see out. The shadows from the trees moving and a branch rubbing against the garden shed at the back of the house is giving her an uncomfortable feeling. She is frozen on the sofa. Narissa rushed downstairs, almost tripping over the last step at the bottom of the stairs but managed to hear her feebly calling out "mumma, where are you?"

Narissa's instinct told her that Maddie had woken up.

Narissa ran up to Maddie, held her like she won't see her again, knowing very well that she will, hugging and kissing her, assuring her that she was not far away. She told Maddie that she was upstairs with her siblings while Maddie was having a nap. Narissa brought a glass of water for Maddie which she gulped it down as if she hadn't had a drink in ages. She didn't feel like eating so they went upstairs, gave her a quick shower and went to read some books in bed.

The other 2 angels have gone to sleep. So it is only 2 of them now, Narissa and Maddie. They read together. Maddie loves her books and Narissa doesn't mind reading till cows come home. This is probably why Maddie started to recognize letters early enough to make a few words and sometimes would make up her own story by looking at the pictures. It is now nearly 6.45pm. Lawrence is late but hey he often is.

Narissa checked on the children, checked that the monitor was on and went downstairs to have dinner. The sound of garage door opening made her very tensed up. Her back stiffened and her shoulder began to rise up to her ears. 'What is he going to do today?' The thought is floating in her head. Whenever Lawrence comes home Narissa feels very uncomfortable.

The door from the hallway to the garage opens and the first words Narissa hears are "why is she up? Shouldn't she be in bed?

He is obviously referring to Maddie. He sometimes speaks as if he hates his children, especially Maddie because she is the oldest, talks the most and seen more.

To cut the long story short I replied "well Maddie was very tired and fell asleep while I was cooking.

"Then she should not be eating right now! She needs to learn not to do this". Lawrence speaks out angrily.

Yeah right!

Anyway, she finished feeding Maddie, loaded the dishwasher while Maddie was happily playing with her soft toys and all Narissa could hear was "but Pappa I want to play".

"No! You are in bed, NOW!" Sounds like Lawrence wants to strangle her.

"Pappa I am not sleepy". Maddie is innocently putting her case forward.

"I don't care". Lawrence shrieks.

Next thing Narissa hears is he is trying to pull her up to bed.

Narissa had to intervene. She grabbed his arm, looked at him in his boiling eyes and calmly whispered "let go. Maddie had a long sleep this afternoon and she has just eaten so she needs to let her food digest. Why don't we eat now and then I will take her to bed later".

No reply.

Anyway, Lawrence disappears upstairs to change from his suit into something comfortable. Narissa doesn't know if she should get dinner warmed up or not. Sometimes she asks and gets told off, sometimes she asks and he says nothing. Narissa stands around waiting for a response.

Maddie decides to put Barney on and they are dancing to "I love you, you love me, and we are a happy family...". All going well.

Lawrence is now downstairs and Narissa asks him how his day was. He replies "usual and what do you want to know?"

She asks if he is ready for dinner. The answer she got tipped me her over. "I had something to eat. The boys all decided to go out and try this new restaurant that opened up".

"Is this the one my brother told us about?" Narissa asked inquisitively.

"No, I dunno". Lawrence responded casually.

Narissa feels a bit deprived and sad. She had refrained herself from going out, indulging in fine foods and spent the day caring for children, housekeeping and worried about spending and he couldn't care less.

So she sat down with Maddie and said "sweetie, mumma needs to eat."

"Why are you eating now? I told you before if I am not home by 6 you should have your dinner." Lawrence speaks in an unsympathetic way.

'Does he even know what was happening at 6pm? Does he even know or care how her day had been?'

Narissa feels hurt. She dearly wanted to go to this new restaurant and now since he has been, it means she will never get to go. She always misses out on everything. It seems so unfair. She has had offers from her mum and friends to baby sit her children while she went out with Lawrence. Yet Lawrence won't accept any offers.

Finally with a sigh, Narissa sat down with her meal and just as she got her first mouthful, Maddie yells out, "mumma I got poo coming." That's all Narissa needed right now.

Unfortunately Maddie needs to go in a hurry and Narissa can see that. Maddie is getting a bit agitated.

"Ask Pappa, darling". Narissa is trying to gulp her food down.

"He is watching TV, Mumma". Maddie is holding her bottom and jumping up and down, swaying from side to side.

Narissa yelled "honey can you take care of Maddie? Maddie is running to the bathroom in the dark hallway and she suddenly stops. "Mumma, I am scared".

Narissa got up to switch the light on in the hallway, and Maddie is on the toilet seat. She has got herself sorted. Narissa tries to simplify everything and make life as easy as possible for herself and the family. She had bought a stool so Maddie can jump on it and reach the toilet seat. There was a little toilet seat insert so that Maddie can sit comfortably without fear of falling into the toilet pan and that means no one has to hold her.

Narissa knew Maddie won't like to stay in this part of the house alone as it was dark and next to the garage door, which scared Maddie a bit, so Narissa stayed with her. She ducked into the laundry which was right next to the toilet and washed her hands, waiting patiently for Maddie to finish.

Maddie was getting good at wiping herself and she always remembered to wash her hands with a lot of soap from the dispenser. If it was day time Maddie would no doubt stay in the bathroom washing her hands forever but it seemed that she was in a hurry. She got back to the lounge and continued with her play.

Narissa started eating again. Half way through her dinner, the monitor goes off. Ella is awake. "Lawrence, can you see what Ella wants?" Narissa speaks with her mouth full. She is trying to gulp her dinner down, washing mouthfuls with water to make her dinner go down faster, and knowing this isn't a good thing.

Did Narissa expect a different answer today? Maybe. Lawrence ignores her as usual.

Narissa had to throw part of her dinner out and it is now 8.30pm. She waited for a few minutes to see if the monitor was giving her false alarms. She quickly started emptying the left overs in a container and getting the dishes into the dishwasher, quickly disinfecting the bench and tidying up the stove area and clearing the bench so that all is ready to go in the morning. There was some clothes to fold and after putting everything away, she was ready to hit the sack.

Except her night never goes smoothly. Everyday Lawrence finds something to argue about. Everyday Narissa lend her ears to listen to his problems at work. Lawrence finds it very difficult to interact with people. He can't form good relationships with people. He also lacks time management and his manager sent him on a course to learn how to manage his time during the day. Lawrence had real problems with the concept of time. He used to put his watches and all the clocks 10 minutes ahead of the actual time, which irritated Narissa a lot.

Narissa had a picture in her head of Lawrence at work. She could see him getting into work, making cups of tea, not knowing where to get started, maybe chatting or tidying up his workspace, running back and forth and then close to end of the day when it is close to 5 o'clock he would be running around trying to get things done.

At home Lawrence was the same. Narissa didn't usually ask him for help but sometimes she had to get some man power help, for instance this project of setting up this swing set she had purchased, was just too heavy for her. First weekend Lawrence's excuse was that he didn't have the right tools. If he didn't have the right tools, wouldn't he be making an effort to get some?

The kids can't wait to use the swing set. Maybe because Narissa made the purchase and not Lawrence himself. Lawrence has this habit of downgrading everything Narissa bought. He would condemn her purchase, he will not be part of it or he won't even acknowledge it.

Anyway, she reminded him on Thursday to bring the tools for the swing set.

"Oh I have them at home." He told her.

On Saturday morning she was willing to give him a hand to build the swing set. Maddie was very keen and Max got his tools out as well. Narissa couldn't lift the box herself so asked Lawrence for help.

"You guys have no patience at all, do you? Look at you all." Lawrence is angrily talking to everyone.

He speaks to the children as if has no desire to see happiness in them at all.

"Don't you think they have waited long enough? Isn't 8 weeks of waiting long enough?" Narissa exclaimed.

Anyway, she didn't want to argue anymore. So she got the kids to break the box and get the parts out, tools out and they were getting excited. Ella begins to skip around while holding Max's hand and Maddie found the instruction sheets and pretended to read the instructions.

Finally they got the pieces of the swing set out and laid the parts on the ground. Narissa started looking at the instructions with Maddie to see what was required. She didn't realise that Lawrence was right behind her. He pulled the instructions out of her hands. "What do you need that for?" in a deep voice to scare them all.

"I was just looking." Narissa exclaimed. Gosh she didn't like his hostility at all.

Lawrence was fluffing around so much, that everyone got bored of watching him place bits here then taking it away. Was he actually trying to complicate it all or was he trying to show everyone that this was a very difficult process. If by the end of the day he has got it together, it meant he was a very clever guy. That's Lawrence's usual self.

Narissa had to leave as she had other thing to take care of and one by one the children all left too. Kids had all gone off to play and Narissa could see that Lawrence was getting agitated. Lawrence wants help but then he starts controlling everyone. "Don't touch that! Don't do that!" "Bring that here, now!" This will continue and besides the children have a short concentration span anyway.

In between all this time Narissa had prepared and served morning tea, lunch, afternoon tea and the children have had their dinner as well. It was quite dark now and Lawrence yelled out, "it is finished! Done!" "I wasted the entire day on building this swing set and they have all gone. No one is here to appreciate all my hard work. No respect and no loyalty."

Turning to me, "Is this what you teach them?"

"Honestly, I don't know what your expectations are. I told you to let go and leave it for another day. The kids are all sleeping. You know what the time is?"

Narissa had fed Lawrence and given him all the help she could in between and the kids have tried to give him a hand but he didn't want their help. He pushed them all out of the way. He was yelling at them a lot and telling them off for touching the bits and moving the screws around.

Lawrence has this brilliant way of pissing everyone off. He can't involve the children when he is doing something. He will yell and boss everyone around and make them all scared of him.

In the past Maddie and Max had tried several times to help Lawrence clean the car and all the time Lawrence will be yelling at them, "Not this way! Don't use up all the water! Idiot!" Max would run away and Maddie would just throw everything and leave angrily.

Maddie got it hard too and wouldn't give him a hand with washing cars anymore.

With Lawrence you are always on a yo-yo. You never know what to do which way to go and whatever you do whether he will be pleased or angry with you.

At times he gives them a smack on their backs or hands and on the face. It is not a light smack, it is usually so hard that it makes Narissa cringe. She can hear it from miles away. Maddie gets angry when that happens and she pushes Lawrence away. I have told the children to stop arguing with dad or when he says not to do something, then just let go. Lawrence starts calling them names, verbally abusing the hell out of them and that's when things don't go well.

*"A smile is a way to solve many problems."*

# CHAPTER 5

*"It is hard to hold tears with my fake smile, still I am doing it because I don't want people to know the reason for my tears.*

'WE ARE HAVING guests over for dinner and I am the culprit since I invited them. I thought it will be nice to have some adult company as I am unable to go out.' Narissa is beating herself up for getting herself into this mass.

Narissa's restrictions run far and high. She cannot go out to movies because it is expensive, she cannot go out for coffee because it means spending money on unnecessary items, when according to Lawrence there is perfectly good coffee at home. Often her cup of tea or coffee is as cold as ice because she forgets to drink it. Two hours later she might pick it up, put it in the microwave to re-heat it. As soon as the microwave beeps, she would run over open the door and close it because she can't drink it right now.

This friend of Narissa is from her University days and they were the best of friends, talking to each other almost every day and till late night some days. Narissa had been out to her family for dinner on several occasions and with Lawrence as well. This time Narissa thought of inviting them over and discovered her brother was visiting from overseas as well. They were all at university together so it will be a very nice catch up. Narissa wanted to cook them something very nice because she doesn't get to do this often enough. She had the menu planned, house cleaned and did some shopping and left the meats for Saturday morning so she could get them fresh. She also needed some fresh herbs. All her herbs were either eaten by snails or slugs, or woody or dead.

They often got mowed over as well. The garden was just a small plot next to the kitchen with nothing of substance growing in them. Most of the plants looked pretty sickly, with thin cotton thread size stems, leaves that were so small you couldn't identify whether it was marjoram or oregano.

The roast leg of lamb with sweet potatoes and vegetables was a perfect meal as Narissa would chuck everything in the oven and get on with dessert, her favourite part of the meal. Pineapple upside down cake drizzled with syrup, covered with moist dates a dollop of ice cream would be very warming. She has to time it all well so that the desert doesn't dry out.

Narissa was frantically doing last minute cleaning. Narissa has this thing that if people's bathroom is clean, then she will know that the residents are clean. She ran to the main bathroom, checked to see if there was enough toilet paper, there isn't any hair on the floor, the towels are all colour coordinated, hung nicely and the shower door is clean and clear as filtered water so you can see through.

Before children arrived in her life Narissa loved entertaining. She had time to try out recipes, take her time to shop, change menus along the week and really look forward to some good laughs. Today she is not.

She can't find Lawrence anywhere and he is supposed to get her some meat. Narissa had everything else organised. She made sure the kids were all fed way before the guests arrive and bathed and settled. It is Saturday but for her every day is the same. She still had to get up early to get the kids breakfast, hubby's breakfast, washing, cleaning, morning tea, lunch and she was hoping to get the roast in by 4.30pm.

It is now 3.30pm and no sight of Lawrence. He must be at the supermarket. She ran downstairs opened the garage door as kids want to have a bike ride, but his car is still in the garage. The yard is not that big so she can't miss him. Oh! She can hear his voice. He is chatting to a neighbour. What surprises her is how long he has been out there chatting when he promised her to get the meat. The leg of lamb her main meal and without this she is done! She can see and feel history repeat itself. It has happened to her before. After the first episode, Lawrence promised that he would never let Narissa down again. Narissa wishes she could do everything herself but she has 2 hands, 2 legs and one body.

'Last time, we had a get together I was a total rack.

Narissa remember the time when she was looking forward to having her token mother for dinner and she ended up with two sick children.'

One was teething and one had severe reaction to something. She ran them down to the local medical centre and had to wait for ages. Max, had rashes and the doctor said it was nothing. He was floppy, not drinking and was asleep most of the time. His ears checked up fine, throat looked fine, his temperature was normal, he was sweaty though.

Ella, had some molars coming through which was hurting and she was miserable, wanted to be close to mumma, extra cuddles, temperature and refusing food or drinks.

After the doctors, Narissa called the Homeopathic Pharmacy and was given advice on a few remedies to take. With no side effect and a gentle cure, she has started to respect this medicine more than ever.

Last get together Narissa didn't get much sleep and she remembers asking for help from Lawrence who just couldn't get his head around the fact that he has to help out in the house. His idea was that a woman's role at home was to raise the children. What he never understood was that her work didn't finish till she went to bed. Narissa started early and finished very late. Lawrence, on the other hand woke up, got dressed, had his breakfast, went to work, went for lunches, coffees and came home to watch TV and went to bed.

Narissa was getting used to not having any physical help and was paying the price by having a body that was crumbling or felt like it sometimes. Emotionally, she was on her own and in hard times, she could only cry silently at night. Even then the tears have stopped coming. There is a cry from inside, bit of sighing and some heart flutters but no tears.

Slowly she was getting the feeling that she was being rejected.

Today, she thought she will interrupt the conversation and see if he could mind the children for at least 30min so she could pop down to the local shopping mall and hopefully don't meet anyone that she knows so she is not compelled to chat. Today she just didn't have the time.

She could have got the leg of lamb the other day while she was getting milk and bread, but it is not that easy. When you have kids with you, all you want to do is grab the necessities and dash to the car.

So here she was waving her arms around from their side of the property over this cedar fence covered in potato vine to grab his attention. She is pretty sure that he is ignoring her. Narissa could see her neighbour trying to step on her toes to give her some height so she can see me. Narissa is only a 5ft 7inches but she can jump.

Her neighbour, Carolyn is trying to tell him that his wife needs attention. Can you believe this? He turns around, looks at Narissa and continues chatting. Is it even possible that he cannot register what his eyes can see? Truly, can he not hear me or see me?

Giving up on this, Narissa went to the side gate, opened the gate and ran to the neighbours, leaving the children in the house. She knows it is only a few minutes but anything can happen even in 2 seconds. So in her hurried speech, slurring with panic in her voice and kind of hyperventilating she managed to spill out "I need to get to the shops, can you mind the children?"

He turned around with the most disgusting look on his face, frown that made the lines on the third eye make 2 equal lines but in a vertical position and the eyes that literally reminded her of a hawk.

"Sorry I had to run like this." Narissa is now telling the neighbour that they have guests arriving shortly.

She realised then that this all makes her look much disorganised. Now she feels like a complete fool and an utterly useless housewife. 'How could I have left all this to the last minute?' she thought.

'Now that I have offered to go means that I have to go and change my clothes which are disgusting from all the cleaning I did plus food scraps from kids fingers and trackies that are fit to be shredded and made into soft toys.'

"Yeah I will be in shortly." hang on what does shortly mean, five minutes, 10 minutes or till one of the kids start screaming or maybe he won't even hear them. He can't usually hear them. His ears are just not tuned into the kids' voices. I am pretty sure he just zones out.

"Do you want to go instead?" She asked very politely.

'Wait, if he goes it means he won't be back for at least 2 hours. Now I feel like saying, well can you at least go now. At the same time I don't want to be that bossy wife.' Narissa thinks.

She ran into the house, rushed her fingers through her hair to straighten it all out. Thank goodness for really short hair at the moment. 'My hair dresser is fantastic! She thought to herself. It' just one of those treats she has remaining in her life. Once in a while Narissa calls this hairdresser who comes home and cuts her hair for $15.00. It involves a quick spray of water all over the head, chop chop and then it is done. Narissa can still see the children and talk to them. Very convenient arrangement.

Narissa is now in the car and Maddie comes running. "Mumma I want to come too." But Maddie might need to go to toilet or she may slow me down. Narissa can't leave her in the house alone since hubby is still chatting. She switched the engine off and gestured for Maddie to come to the car. Then she saw Max peeking through the door. Her motherly instincts are too strong. She yelled at Max to come in to the car. As she lifted Max up to put him into his car seat, she realised that his diaper was soaked with urine. Thankfully they make diapers to hold a lot of liquid and also to soak up the odour.

'Should I go and change him.' Narissa is thinking. It means leaving Maddie in the car alone.

No choice, she took Maddie out of the car, explaining that Max needs a diaper change. Carried Max up the stairs to change his diaper. If he walked he would have taken forever. A quick change of diaper and then they are on their way. She went downstairs and Maddie had managed to soak her dress with orange juice. She wanted some juice and managed to spill it all over herself. Okay, it is not her fault and what else could she do while waiting? When Maddie wants something it usually means now and hurried. Narissa guessed that Maddie must have decided to hurry along and misjudged her pouring capacity. At least there aren't any broken glasses to clean or the whole juice bottle on the floor. Things could be worse.

'Maybe I am being slowed down for a good reason, expecting hubby to appear from the back door any minute. But that's hoping for a miracle.'

Still no sign of Lawrence.

Quick change of dress for Maddie, now both in the car seat, seat belts in and Narissa needs to pee.

As she pulled out of the driveway, she can still hear Lawrence chatting. She reversed out onto the road now and slowly driving past the neighbour's house. She caught a glimpse of Lawrence, chatting away, looking happy and smiles from ear to ear, nodding and making gestures like he is obviously bragging about something. Narissa put her car windows down and screamed out that Ella was still sleeping and she has Maddie and Max in the car her. He looked even happier. Why can't he be this happy at home? He is always grumpy and yelling at everyone at home.

Did he do this purposely? Did he try to get out of going shopping or looking after the children? He takes no responsibility whatsoever!

Narissa finally got to the supermarket and explained to the children that mummy doesn't have much time so this is a real quick shopping day. What do they know about time? Max wants to walk or push the trolley. Both kids are holding hands and slowly making their way to the supermarket. At this stage Narissa thinks what if there was a cooked lamb of leg available. 'I could cheat, but I want to impress my friends so no I shouldn't have thoughts like this.' Anyway this sort of service hasn't started at Woollies or Coles yet.

She got her leg of lamb and now Maddie wants a toy and Max has grabbed a few extra items. Narissa is not in the mood nor have the emotional strength to argue. They left the shopping mall and got home, quickly unpacked all the shopping and the kids are happy with their purchases. At least they are busy. New toys always keeps them engaged for a little while. Hopefully, Lawrence doesn't see this new purchase today. Even if he didn't the kids would let him know anyway.

Narissa quickly dressed this leg of lamb, rubbing rosemary, crushed ginger, bit of soy sauce, making little cuts so the sauce can penetrate the meat fibres. Chucked it in the oven. The rest of the vegetables were all ready to go in and then she has to get the upside down cake to prepare.

She heard the baby upstairs. Where is hubby? "Honey can you get Ella?" "She is ok".

"Actually, she has been sleeping for a while so she needs attention. Can you please bring her down?"

Narissa turned around and Max has got paint all over his fingers and he is having a grand old time spreading it on his white kiddie table. The look on his face is like a little monster, knowing mummy is busy and he goes to put on a display with colours that you would not have seen before. The thick texture of the bright reds and blues are melting in his tiny fingers and dripping like melted chocolate. He is so engrossed in his little task that he can't see Narissa starring at him.

She took some deep breaths and sat on the floor next to him. The table top is just below her shoulders and she can comfortably reach out. She looked at Max again and this time she noticed that he has a smile on his face stretching out from ear to ear.

He doesn't have a clue regarding time, regarding mummy's anxiety, he is just being a child. Then he says "mumma play? It's mummy's turn now. He tries to splash some paint on Narissa and she was totally speechless for a few minutes.

"Max, mumma can't play sweetie. Mumma has work to do. Remember Aunty and uncle are coming for dinner?"

What does he know about that? Max couldn't care less. 'Sometimes, I love the innocence in children'. Narissa thought to herself and catching a little smile and a flutter in her heart. It gave her a lot of joy to see her children happy.

So like a good mother should, she left him to his own imagination. This play won't last for long anyway. She has the patience of a true fisherman, she can wait till he has finished.

In the meantime Maddie decides to bring the baby down. Ella is wrapped in shawls half dangling and what freaked Narissa out was how did she come down the stairs at age 5, with baby in her arms and the shawl loosely around Ella with bits hanging on the floor.

Narissa's heart missed a beat. She had no time to think. She screamed out "how did the baby get here?" She then rushed over to Maddie and checked on Ella. Everything looked fine. Ella was smiling, looking up at Maddie's face. She was trying to touch Maddie's face with her tiny soft fingers. Narissa didn't want to scare Maddie by over reacting. "Maddie sweetie, when your arms start to ache you tell Mumma, ok?"

"We will then, put Ella in the cot." Narissa explained.

Can things get any worse around here?

Narissa sighed and let off some pant up air before putting on some soothing music and followed by putting some drinks in the fridge. She had to prepare the entree plate. 'We are just having some cheese, breads, and crackers, sun dried tomatoes, olives, antipasto and dips. I did make some spring rolls but haven't made any sauce. Sweet chilli sauce out of a bottle bought at the supermarket will do.'

Narissa got all the cutlery out for tonight and hopefully no one touches them because she made sure they don't have fingerprints on them.

Narissa is learning to let go of a lot of things. She is beginning to be less fussy and sometimes doesn't bother to tidy up the lounge. She had been reading a lot of self-help books and is learning a house is to be lived in. It is not a show home.

Ella is ready for a feed and she can't hold it any longer. She is now sucking on Maddie's thumb and we don't even know if they are clean. Maddie has a tendency to pick her nose and pat the cats and Narissa doesn't even know if she washed her hands before picking up Ella.

Ella sucks on it for a bit and then gives out an awful cry of help and you hear her making noises to get some juice out of Maddie's thumb. Maddie can't handle it as it is beginning to hurt so she tries to give another finger.

Gosh 'I cannot settle down to feed till I have fixed Max. I can't leave him like this. He will put colour on everything he touches.'

'My problem is that I allow kids to be kids. Other people would call that naughtiness.' How is that even naughty?

Anyway, she can now hear Lawrence coming in and pulling Max out of the chair. Narissa automatically goes into a high alert mode whenever she hears or feels Lawrence coming.

"What are you doing? You stupid kid. Look what you have done, ruined the table?" Lawrence is shouting at Max and he turns to Narissa "you don't even stop him? What kind of a mother are you? No wonder kids have no discipline." He adds.

Seriously, discipline? Is that what he calls discipline? Not allowing them to be kids. Poor Max is being dragged down to the bathroom, one arm strongly held by Lawrence's strong manly arms who has no clue how gentle Max's soft muscles and tender joints are. Max falls to the floor and he just drags him.

Not able to tolerate the harshness in Lawrence, she rushes out to protect Max as this is abuse to her. What she sees horrifies her even more.

He is pulling and pushing Max to the ground. Narissa had no choice but to butt in. "Let go! Can you not see he is hurting?" 'Well he shouldn't have been playing with paint like that."

Max looked totally scared and couldn't even open his mouth

to say anything. He just made little groaning noises. He lay on the floor motionless.

Narissa got hold of Max and just gave a hug and then got him to the bathroom, got him undressed and ran the bath. Max wouldn't look at Narissa, his eyes down to the floor and just followed Narissa's instructions. He didn't cry and didn't say a word. Narissa hugged him again and told him that Max made a bit of a mass but that's how he played with paint and that Daddy had never seen him play with paint before and didn't know

We don't need much water in the bath. I managed to wash most of the paint off in the bathroom sink. I can see the red marks on his arm from the pressure of the man handle.

In the meantime Ella cannot hold it anymore. She is screaming and Maddie cannot control her anymore. She is screaming for help.

"Maddie! Mummy is busy. Are you blind?" is Lawrence's response.

I don't get it. Can he not help? Can he do anything right? Why can't he take Ella off Maddie's arms? She has been holding him for a while now.

I got Max in the bath and left him for a few seconds alone to get the baby. I sat next to the bath, on a stepping stool and got Ella onto the nipple. She is now gasping and gaping, making slurpy noises to get the milk flowing. Gosh it hurts. I have been stressed so it take a few minutes for milk to flow. Be patient Ella. I feel so bad but what to do. I am so divided among the children.

I feel exhausted and I don't want to entertain anymore. If only I could call it a day now.

Ella is feeding now and she is happy. My other breast if filling up now. I can't change but to let it fill up. The breast is now so tender. The mistakes I made with Maddie, won't happen with Ella. I used to move her from side to side. But she probably only got the fore-milk which was full of sugar etc. and not enough hind milk which had more fats and sustainable food.

Ella needs to burp and she lets go of the nipple. I have her up facing me now and gently rest her on my shoulders. Max wants to come out. Usually I have to hurry them out of the bath but today I want him to stay in there a bit longer. I want to keep him occupied in the bath till I finish with Ella.

Max is very good natured. He will listen and he happily continued to play. Ella was huge feeder and since the milk from the right breast was finished, I had to latch her on the left one. Off she goes. I have no idea of time and I have no idea of what's happening in the oven.

Felt like two hours had passed on and Maddie comes up. "Mumma I am hungry."

"Where's dad, Maddie?" "He is watching TV and said don't disturb me. Mumma I am really hungry."

I know Maddie very well. She won't come to me till she was really desperate. So I told her to go downstairs and there is some spring rolls, crackers and dips that she can have. I thought that will hold her for a bit.

Finally Ella is fed and happy as. Max is out of the bath and ready to put clothes on.

Downstairs is not so happy. Maddie is now being told off for eating from the guest's food. I can hear her protesting. My poor darling gets so much flack for just being herself. How cruel is this man. If she doesn't listen, he will clip her ears, pull her arm and push and shove her like she is an object.

Here I go...I am downstairs defending my darling Maddie. "Just talk to her nicely and she will get it. There's no need to be so harsh and cruel. She is a child." As if he can't see that. "Anyway, since you won't get off your arse, I asked Maddie to help herself from the plate on the kitchen bench. I gave her permission."

"Well I didn't know."

"You could have asked Maddie if she was allowed."

This has taken me years to understand. There is a certain kind of brain that thinks differently to a normal person. Normal people will say "Maddie, who gave you permission to eat from that plate?"

Or they might say "Maddie, did mummy say you can have that?" Now I call that love and respect.

Unfortunately, this type of brain will see something and automatically react. Doesn't matter what the situation is. They cannot think of reasons why someone will be doing what they are doing. In this case his brain says "Maddie is stealing."

Explain that! "For heavens sakes Maddie is not stealing! I gave her permission to eat from the plate. She was hungry and you wouldn't respond to her needs and the easiest solution was to allow her to help herself from the plate."

For fucks sake, do I have to explain all this every time something happens?

In our house, YES. Because someone needs explanations all the time. They cannot see beyond the horizon and they cannot reason, and they are always right!

"Sometimes humour makes reasoning unjustified"

# CHAPTER 6

*"The informality of family life is a blessed condition that allows us to become our best while looking our worst."* —**Marge Kennedy**

7.30AM AND MADDIE is packed with excitement, like a balloon freshly filled with helium on a string, dancing to melodies of our radiating energy. A totally inflated balloon standing upright on a string. Maddie is however like a lose balloon, reaching for the sky.

Last night she found it difficult to sleep. Narissa read books to Maddie, maybe one book approximately three times, from front cover to the back. Patience is her strongest pain but she was feeling a bit scattered inside because of the uncertainty of getting everything together in the morning. She had lunch box to prepare, two little children to get organised and get Maddie to school. Often, only one child needs to do something out of kilter and time needs to stop for ten to thirty minutes, except it doesn't. It seems Narissa was always in a catch up mode but you never catch up.

She sang and told some made up stories, which she became an expert at. Narissa could make stories as she went because her mind worked faster than her mouth. When Maddie was finally asleep, Narissa crawled into bed to a snoring blob of human flash. Lawrence took a lot of space even in a big king sized bed.

She often felt that she was sleeping on the edge and about to fall off the bed.

'Maybe I don't sleep all night and that's why I wake up so unrefreshed'. Narissa was thinking to herself. Last time she saw her Homeopath, Narissa told her that she slept well without thinking about it. The lies she had given, no wonder she was beginning to lose confidence in them. The truth is she don't know the truth!

'I jump out of bed, 7.00am on the clock. Wholly crap! I slept in on the first day of my daughters' school? What kind of a mother does that? My mind works on overtime every time so I quickly hop in the shower. I can manage a 10 second shower'. Narissa is panicking now.

"Calm down, take some deep breaths and carry on." she told herself. She quickly put on some jeans, a t-shirt and ran down the hallway to see who else was up. They are all up. This leaves her no time to empty the dishwasher, feed the cats, and make the lunch box which is half prepared.

'I can't forget any of my chores because like your past, it will hunt me down at the end of the day. It can cause havoc with my time and I will not cope well.' Narissa tells herself and half talking loud.

She ran downstairs to feed the cats, change the water in the cat bowls and while she was down there, she noticed a puddle of water.

'Crap! Is this cat piss? No, the smell is not strong enough for that. Is it the washing machine leaking? I hope not.' Narissa cannot stand till and fret over it. Something has to be done. Then she remembered, she did some washing last night which had to be put on the line. Takes 20 minutes or more of her time because all the clothes are small and fiddly. Sometimes it feels like she has spent an hour at the clothesline. Such a painful task.

The water on the floor might have been when she rinsed Max's t-shirt and transferred to the washing machine. With that thought, she ran upstairs to check on the children.

Maddie was ready for breakfast, waiting patiently at the little table. Narissa put her clothes on the edge of the bed last night so she could get up and dress herself. The bag was packed with spare change of clothes, two pairs of knickers and her book and a pencil case. The pencil case that had Barbie all over and the bag with several pockets that Maddie decided to put extra toys in, without Narissa's consultation. 'We have a battle on our hands. Anyway, no point saying anything right now because she will just get agitated.' thought Narissa.

First things first, breakfast. Usually it is oats with some sliced bananas, honey, nuts, and dried fruits in a warm milk. Sometimes Maddie likes to have scrambled eggs but Narissa is always chasing the tail of time. Oh oh! Maddie is not wearing the clothes they had on the bed for her. She decides to wear what was in the school bag. Only one thing to do, put the clothes she was meant to wear back into the school bag and take unnecessary items out.

Maddie at the table, eating, time to find Max. He is usually jumping off the coffee table or in his bedroom jumping off the bed and tables. He has got his top back to front and the inside vest is over his top. He has changed the diaper himself and I wonder where the used one is. Max is actually trying to brush his teeth in the bathroom, standing over the vanity on the little stool Narissa had purchased at a 2 buck store. "What a clever boy!" she exclaimed.

"Max, breakfast for you, sweetie?"

He says "not now", feeling like a grown up boy, standing on a bathroom stool and he had toothpaste on his toothbrush. Time is ticking and it is already after 8am. Sometimes Maddie mothers Max and it is quite nice as it frees Narissa up.

Where is Lawrence? He said he was going to help out this morning by taking Maddie to school. Narissa cannot see him anywhere. She hopes he is in the downstairs study just waiting for everyone to get ready.

Narissa walks towards the babies' room and can hear Ella playing in her room. Thank goodness she doesn't have breast milk anymore. That saves a lot of time. Quick change and Ella is ready for her breakfast. They make their way to the kitchen picking up Max along the way. He is as happy as a little prince on his first day out to the woods. He has smile beaming across his face. Max is a little chubby but very cute. His dark curly hair falls on his forehead and at the sides and he often tucks the hair behind his ears. Everyone calls him handsome and his dimples make him super cute. They say that boys are their mother's apple of the eye and the girls are the princesses of their fathers. 'Wish I could say that about my girls.' Narissa felt hard in her chest.

Max is at the table and Ella is on her high chair and both being fed. Narissa still has to feed Ella. Her food can be a lose canon, therefore on a busy morning it is better for Narissa to be in charge here. Her food sometimes fly's and finds its way into Maddie or Max's bowl. Ella thinks it is a lot of fun and so do Maddie and Max which makes it worse because it encourages Ella to do more.

Narissa is finishing off the lunch box, making sure she puts Maddie's water bottle in. She got Maddie to put her lunch box and water in her bag herself so she knows exactly where everything is when she is at school. Maddie notices that some of her 'things' like mummy's t-shirt and her favourite book is not in it. She questions Narissa as if she was her mother. "Muuum." With that tone I know we have a problem. "Yes, baby". "Where are my things from the bag?" she asks very sternly with pouty lips and a frown.

"What things?" Narissa replies sounding like she didn't know.

"I had my book in here. Ri-ght he-re. In this pocket". She has a bloody good memory.

"Oh Maddie, since it is your fav-vourite book, I took it out, be-cause I didn't want it to get lost at school." Narissa replied in an apologetic voice.

"No-oooo, I will not take it out of the bag!" Maddie replied again sternly.

"What if someone else takes it?" Narissa is trying to be empathetic.

"Muuuum, no one will take it. I know that." Replied Maddie stomping her feet.

Narissa left and noticed that Maddie had put the book and the t-shirt inside the middle pocket of her cute little Barbie bag. Narissa realised how clever Maddie was. By putting them in the middle pocket she will eliminate the chances of getting it stolen by opportunists.

Maddie has been carrying this t-shirt of Narissa's since she came out of hospital when she was sick at age three and found herself displaced. Even though Narissa had done everything to make sure that she didn't. Max had arrived and Maddie who was full of excitement and joy before the baby's arrival, had gone into remission. Even though she loved her brother to bits, she couldn't stand how mummy was forever paying attention to Max.

Maddie got really high temperature, was taken to hospital and admitted because the doctors thought she might have had chicken pox and needed to be isolated. Narissa had ticked the box which said Maddie had been in contact with someone with Chicken pox. Maddie was extremely irritated by all the fuss at the hospital. The doctors had no idea what was going on so they tried to make her pee in a pouch they attached to a diaper. They thought she might have bladder infection. Maddie was toilet trained and hated being in the diaper, let alone the uncomfortable pouch.

Since the night at the hospital, Maddie carried this t-shirt everywhere in the house. She never took it out of the house. Today was the first time she was taking it out and of all places, to school. Maddie obviously wants to feel close to mum and Narissa had to let it go. She might just have to mention to the teachers at school.

'We have to leave home around 8.30', thought Narissa. She started looking for Lawrence.

"Maddie, do you want to see if dad is ready to take you?" Narissa asked Maddie who already had her back pack and shoes on.

Just then Narissa heard Lawrence "Bye everyone, see you after work."

Narissa quickly ran towards the voice "Aren't you taking Maddie to school?" she exclaimed.

"Oh no I can't. I have a meeting and need to leave now." Lawrence replied casually.

"Didn't you say last night that you were?" Narissa is getting into a panicky mood.

"Well yeah, but this guy wants to meet at 9a.m." Lawrence replied as if it is not a big deal.

"But you said you will drop Maddie on your way to work!" Narissa was almost shouting.

"Pappa, I can't miss school, it is my first day." Maddie said in her sweetest softest voice.

"I know, Maddie but Pappa has a meeting." Lawrence replies again very casually while putting his shoes on.

When did this meeting happen? Narissa really wonders how he can change like a chameleon. Last night he said he was helping. This morning 10 minutes before he is supposed to leave home he tells her he can't.

Her body begins to heat up, blood is boiling, and her blood pressure must have skyrocketed. She hadn't planned to do this. Max and Ella have swimming lessons at 9.30am.

'How can he do this? Doesn't he have any empathy? Doesn't he know what he is putting me through right now? I have to pack Max and Ella's water bottles and snacks.' Narissa is feeling dizzy with all the thoughts jumping in her head.

Luckily, the swimming gear was already packed up in the bags from last lesson. Had she not been so organised, it would have been impossible to do anything with the children.

'How can he tell me now? What was he doing all this time?' Narissa was feeling really weak, angry and really let down.

She wanted to just melt down.

This is how his brain works. He was sitting on his computer in the study, chatting to mates at work. Somebody says "how far away are you? You want to do coffee?" "Yeah I will be there, man." No commitment, no responsibilities, no empathy.

Suddenly he is on his way, on his way to work. His work is 10 min from Maddie's school. Maddie is looking horrified. "Pappa, don't leave me!" her arms are stretched out wide.

"Oh darling, I will take you tomorrow."

Well this is normal too. Everything is tomorrow, not today.

Narissa looked at him, her eyes are beginning to fill with tears and she was sweating, her head felt full and her heart felt hard. She was frozen. A heavy bucket from the crane had fallen on her. She looked at Maddie and felt the sadness in her. Narissa grabbed her stretched out arms and hugged. "Mumma will take you." Maddie is so grown up. She says "but mumma you are busy."

"No darling, Max and Ella will come too." How am I to manage this today? I feel like I am going to pass out and can feel blood leaving my body.

She got water for Max and Ella, grabbed some snacks and chucked the bags and ran down the stairs. The least he could have done was helped pack the bags or carry them down for her.

She got Max and Maddie to go downstairs and wait in the garage. The internal access door was open and the car was unlocked. Narissa was carrying, two bags, a child and making sure she had turned everything off, rush off downstairs and Maddie was trying to put Max's seatbelt on. She went past the study and there he was, on the phone laughing his head off, "yeah mate, just got held off at home. You know what it's like with kids."

'Really? He hasn't contributed a bit this morning and never does. What is he going on about?' Narissa thought.

"I will be there in 10." He added.

'In 10?' she thought.

Didn't he say he had a meeting at 9 and had to leave straight away? What happened then?

This is what baffles her about his character. He sees Narissa and starts talking seriously.

"Yeah, I have got the proposal, which I worked on all night. We can discuss this over coffee. Nah I haven't had time for breakfast. You know very busy morning with kids. My oldest is starting school so yeah. Yeah mate, you can imagine" Lawrence keeps chatting.

'What on earth is this crap? I can't believe what I am hearing. I just stared at him' Narissa just kept starring as if in a trance.

He quickly rampaged through some paper, picked up his computer bag, and to Narissa "I will be late for my meeting".

All she could do was swallow, empty heavy air. The swallowing was making her throat uncomfortable. She didn't finish her tea. She ate half a piece of toast and he was saying he had a busy morning with kids?

'Someone, explain that to me? Right now I want to put a knife through his stomach because my stomach is churning acid right now' Narissa was saying in her head.

Seriously, she didn't understand this at all. She had everyone in the car. She put her foot on the accelerator and just moved the car at a speed that felt like her body had left the car. Maddie felt abandoned as she looked out the window to see her daddy getting into his car with his computer case, phone stuck to his ears, in this fancy suit. She said quietly 'bye Pappa."

Narissa's heart was pounding and he just has no idea. The lies were getting to Narissa. The lies he tells other people and everyone he meets forms an opinion about him that is so far removed from reality.

Narissa tried to cheer everyone up. She found a park outside the school and Maddie grabbed her bag. She had to get everyone out of the car and walk down the path to find Maddie's classroom. Ella in her arms greeting other mothers with gleeful smiles along the way. Maddie was making eye contact with a lot of kids but holding Max's hand firmly. As they were walking down the path past the playground, Ella held Narissa's breast and says "milk". Narissa realised then that she had forgotten to put on her bra. Both breasts were soft and saggy after three rounds of breastfeeding. She was very embarrassed. She thought to herself that Ella was better off being carried in her arms because no one will notice. But Ella thought it was funny. She would squeeze her breasts and chuckle and Narissa not wanting any attention drawn to herself had to quicken her pace and keep moving.

Maddie had no trouble settling in. They left her at the door, had a brief chat to her class teacher who was a lovely young vibrant young lady in her mid-thirties. She was beautifully groomed and a smile that will make the children feel loved.

Narissa breathed a sigh of relief.

After swimming lesson, she got home and emptied the swimming bags, washed the towels, togs and goggles. The towels were in the washing machine spinning. The clothes were still wet and she added just more to it. After feeding the children, and playing with them, she put Max in his cot for an afternoon nap. Ella didn't always have a nap. She wanted Narissa to read to her. They read one book and then she was off again. Chucked her half eaten hard piece of bread from this morning in the bin, tea down the sink and made another cup. She realised how thirsty she was. What she really felt like was nice cold water or a juicy fruit.

As soon as she picked up an orange, she remembered what Lawrence had said last week and many weeks before. He reminded Narissa that she was spending too much money on fruits and vegetables. So she glanced at the fruit bowel, one more orange left.'

Maybe I will have this one and leave one' thinking while slicing the oranges into eight pieces and took a slice to the mouth. She tried to suck the juice out of one slice and her stomach started feeling full. She had no desire to finish the rest and felt guilty of eating this one whole orange. She forced herself to eat another slice and stopped after the fourth one. She left the other four in case one of the kids want it later. In this way, she will have a whole one left in the fruit bowl. She felt better at that thought.

*"Guilt: the gift that keeps on giving". Erma Bombeck*

# CHAPTER 7

*"The grass is greenest where it is watered"*

I T IS SPRING time, the daffodils are out in the garden and the winter days are getting longer which means kids have bit more time outside in the sun. Suddenly the sun's rays feel warmer on the cheeks. Everyone seems to be chirpy and cheery. I love spring, the flowers the new shoots on the trees, the spring lambs and just the freshness of the soil, the grass, the atmosphere and the clean fresh feel. It feels like fresh crisp linen filled with lavender smell rubbing against the softness of the cheeks on a new born baby. Every tree has blossoming buds with tiny speckles of leaves forcing its way out of the stems to see the new beginning.

'I feel the need to do something with my time and life; undertake studies or a hobby to challenge my now unstimulated, stagnant brain. The reality is that I am missing adult company and need to move away from just doing all children's stuff. Don't get me wrong, I really enjoy my time with my children but sometimes it is nice to hear another adult's point of view.' Narissa is sitting on the back deck, just reminiscing her working days.

Although Narissa talks to the children and is often challenged by all their questions; how to answer each question depends at the level of their understanding; choosing the words so children can understand

and thinking way ahead before she answers puts a lot of pressure on her as well. With the adults she doesn't have to make stories up, she can be honest and speak her mind regarding adult matters.

'Sometimes I just want to be me, meaning I have the need to just speak out as words flow into my brain. How do you explain 'delicious'? I move my tongue around my lips lick my lips and roll my eyes. To an adult I can say 'delicious' or 'delicimo' and no more explanation required.'

Reading the paper is a rare occasion for Narissa and usually she reads one paper over many nights. Sometimes she flicks through, reads the headlines and take quick glimpses at the adverts that are of concern to her and then the paper disappears under the cat litter box.

She was ruffling through the newspaper and an advert grasped her eyes. There was a course for people who want to get into their own businesses. She looked at the email address and copied it straight into her head. She had to write the phone number down, but ripped the paper around the small outline of the advert and stuck it in her eye glass case. It was a small advert but obviously meant to capture Narissa.

It took her a few days before she could actually do a search and look into this course. She called the phone number that was on the paper and received a very warm welcome from the receptionist. She explained the course time table, which was one evening per week, taught by people in the respective industries. For example, the topic on finance was taught by someone from the finance department in government.

Narissa was very excited and decided to enrol in it. After all, it was just one night from 6pm-9pm per week and 16 weeks altogether. At the end of it she will get a Certificate in small business management.

The difficult part was talking to Lawrence about it. She found it very difficult to discuss anything with Lawrence. If he didn't have an interest in anything, then he didn't want to know about it. If it concerned Narissa or the children he didn't want to know about it. In fact discussing with Lawrence was not a done thing.

One day she picked up the courage to bring the subject of studying with Lawrence and his response was all good. He said not a problem, whatever you want to do. This surprised Narissa but she didn't think that Lawrence had comprehended what she had said. He is always absorbed in his own thoughts and she has always felt emotionally much unsupported. She was explaining it to him regarding the course location, which was ten minutes' drive from home and the contents. He was very interested and Narissa thought for once he was actually listening and truth be known, she felt really good about it.

Her first class was starting in 4 weeks and she felt butterflies in her stomach. Narissa hadn't studied in 7 years. What if she cannot remember anything that she read? What if she unable to understand the contents? What if she falls asleep in class? To her classmates she didn't want to be known as a housewife or a housekeeper. She wanted to be intelligent and she liked the term "Domestic engineer." She wondered if there were other housewives in this course.

Narissa rang the institute again and asked them what sort of age group this course was for and what was the failure rate. Very pleased with the answer, she decided that it will be fun.

The class started at 6.15pm and finished at 9pm. This meant that there was no time for a lot of socialising with the class mates. First night of her class she was already late by 15 minutes.

The day of her class, she got everything organised, even practised her hand writing. She had a small satchel with her pencil case with kids felt tip pens, some pencils, a pen and most importantly her reading glasses. She had these pair since she left work and presume they were still good to use. She couldn't afford the Optometry because Lawrence kept saying that he didn't have any money for all her extravagant spending. Dental was only done when she was in severe pain.

Narissa was super dooper at organising the household. She had her dinner, fed the children, made sure they will be well behaved for Lawrence. She laid her clothes on the bed as though she was going on a date, even though she was only putting on a pair of jeans and a T-shirt. She took a cardigan just in case she would get cold as it can happen in lecture rooms.

After all the fretting and preparations for weeks, she still managed to get into class late. The introductions had already happened, the course outline, text material, contact details of the lecturers and all the material had been handed in. There was one space left for her right in the front row and Narissa had no choice but to sheepishly take seat and grab the paper works later. She felt humbly inadequate and shy.

What happened to once very confident woman, who could walk in a room full of people and start making jokes and conversation to the person next to her?

She remembers going to school assemblies and immediately making conversations with people right next to her. She remembers walking into conference rooms, workshops and never feeling this low and horribly empty.

'Am I just not prepared for this?' thought Narissa.

She was sitting in this classroom with people dressed in suits, some in casual clothes, like herself as they had all come from different activities. Some had come straight from work, some were stay-at-home mums and dads, unemployed and from the corporate world, such a mixture.

Narissa couldn't focus on what the lecturer was saying. Her head began to spin, the room was feeling dark and she felt as if she would pass out. One of the things she remembers from reading all the self-help and healing books is to take deep breaths and put positive affirmations in your head. She started to take some deep breaths but not being too loud so person next to her would think she was having an asthma attack. She was merely getting some air into her lungs. She kept reminding herself "I can do this. I can focus and I am here to learn."

'I am thinking that because I am with the children all day, I am speaking with mums and having small talks at the shops with shop assistants, maybe I am not in tune with this language the tutor is speaking in. It feels very foreign. All I hear is a voice but words don't mean a thing.' Narissa was overwhelmed.

She picked up her pen and started doodling, this usually brings things down a bit. She lifted her head up and saw the tutor looking at her with suggestive eyes.

'Shit! Did he ask me something?' Narissa thought and looked straight at him and had a look on her face that said "I am paying attention." Her eyes were darting upper left then down, blinked a few times, her eyebrow raised one side and down again. Yes, she was thinking but not what he is thinking. Her mind was far away, analysing everything about home.

Finally she was beginning to get grounded. The tutor brought all the papers he had handed in to the class before her late arrival, he showed her the contents and the dates of all assignments due, contact details of all the upcoming tutors and course work expectations. 'Wholly crap! This is a lot of work and commitment.' Narissa thought hoping she hadn't overcommitted herself.

Time for a break. 'Already? I just got here.' She thought.

Anyway, everyone gets up as Narissa was trying to file things into her folder. She really didn't want to mess this up. She should go into the kitchen and meet some people. This is who she is, likes meeting people. Lawrence always hated this in her. Narissa could make conversations with anyone, anywhere, any time and had a good sense of humour. She would make jokes with people she didn't know but that was just her friendly nature. She didn't always get attached to people and start taking phone numbers down. Lawrence liked that in her when they were first dating. He just didn't like it after they got married.

When she had met Lawrence she felt that he loved her for who she was, the friendly, independent, outgoing natured. After a while he started copying Narissa. He would make such stupid mistakes that made her feel small and he would start saying things to strangers like "oh I should get your number and maybe you could come over for dinner one day," as if he was going to cook.

'No! I don't know these people and I don't like the conversation I am having so why get too close. He doesn't understand how to sieve people.' Since their marriage Lawrence became a very jealous man. Every man Narissa talked to became my 'boyfriend', she couldn't share a joke or laugh with anyone any more.

Narissa made her way to the kitchen and made herself a cup of tea, grabbed a cookie and went to where all the other students were congregated. "Hi" looking around sheepishly, "sorry if I disturbed you all by coming in late." They all responded by saying it didn't matter. One lady thought she had trouble finding a car park, but you couldn't, not in this place. This was a building with its own parking space for over a hundred cars. There was plenty of parking space. One guy believed she had family issues. How could he tell that? Anyway, she didn't exchange any phone numbers. Just listening to everyone she realised most of them knew each other through work or were friends and wanted to get into businesses together. Narissa was the only one on her own, not that it bothered her.

The class resumed and she felt a bit better. Taking notes was difficult as her fingers were not gripping the pen very well. She was frantically trying to take notes when the lecturer came over and said, "We have all of these notes in this blue booklet. I am going through this booklet and you can make notes in them." In other words Narissa didn't have to write down everything he was saying. 'How dumb of me that I didn't see this blue booklet and everyone else was sitting and listening. OMG! I am feeling like a real dumb kid today.'

At the end of the evening she couldn't wait to run out of the classroom but at the same time she was beginning to enjoy the course content. The lecturer was very articulate, smart and in total control of himself.

After the class, as she was picking up her books and pens and packing her bag, the lecturer appeared. "Hi, I am Dr Timothy and I am here for the next 4 weeks. My phone number is on the list at the back of this book and if you need any help, please do not hesitate to contact me. If I do not answer, leave a message with the best time to call you and I will return your call. My email address is also there and please feel free to throw any questions at me." He spoke so clearly and in such a gentle manner that Narissa could just smooch him right now.

'How nice of him to pay so much attention to me! I haven't received this attention in a long time.' she thought. She was feeling young and rejuvenated again.

Something told her that she was going to enjoy this course. She felt really supported like a little girl learning to ride a bike for the first time with her dad. That feeling of being safe and supported, 'yes I can do this', she thought. 'Thank you, thank you.' she said it to herself in her head.

She didn't want to behave like a teenage girl and go over the top with thank you. So she replied politely "that's very kind of you and thank you for your support." Narissa didn't look into his eyes either in case she got tongue tied. She kept packing her stuff away while thanking him and nodding her head.

He must have said this to the class when Narissa was still on the road or parking her car and running up the stairs like a lost duckling.

Driving home was a demise. Narissa's head was full of new information and homework to do. There was a lot of reading to do before the next class. She got home, feeling exhausted. Her head felt full. She hadn't studied like this since she left university. All she wanted to do was just go home to a nice cosy bed to sleep.

She opened the garage door slowly and walked through the internal access door very quietly, almost tip toeing so not to wake anyone up. It was 9.20pm and all the kids would be fast asleep. No need for lights as she can make her way through the house to her bedroom. She knows every step, every wall and door in the house.

Narissa got to the top of the stairs and Maddie calls out "MUUUUM" in a soft loud whisper.

"My goodness Maddie, why aren't you in bed yet?" Narissa responded quickly and whispering aloud.

"Well, I had to read this book and dad fell asleep while I was reading. So no one heard me read and I can't get him to sign. I tried to wake him and he shouted at me. He said to shut up and leave him alone, so I did." Maddie is telling her story with the cutest tone, her lips curling up and moving around which made Narissa reach out and hug her tightly.

She went along with Maddie to her bedroom and found Lawrence fast asleep in Maddie's bed, taking all the space on this king-single bed and snoring his lungs out. The bedside light was still on.

Narissa had to wake Lawrence up by giving him a little nudge and shaking him gently. Lawrence wakes up shaking himself and first thing he does, "Maddie, what are you doing still up?"

"But dad, you are in my bed!" Maddie yells out.

"Did you finish your book?"

"Yes, but you didn't listen!"

"Stop shouting!" Lawrence is getting agitated.

"I am so exhausted and I have an early start." This is typical Lawrence every day. He always has an early start as if no one else does.

Disgusted with his behaviour, Narissa assured Maddie that she will sign the book and then she can sleep.

"Mummy, the teacher said someone has to listen to me read. You can't sign yet."

"Maddie, it is very late and can we do it in the morning?" Narissa pleads with Maddie.

"No, Mummy. You are busy in the morning." Maddie is sounding it like a teacher, taking her time to spit out each word.

"How about you read when I am making sandwiches." Narissa is trying to speed up the process. It is very late for Maddie.

Narissa knows that Maddie has this habit of getting things done when they are supposed to be done. She won't rest till she has finished her task. This is a good thing, I guess. It is teaching her some very good life lessons. Narissa can also see the point that if she signed the book without listening to her read, then she was teaching her to cheat. That's not a good life lesson. She had to make a quick decision in three seconds and said "Ok Maddie, you read from where you finished with dad."

Narissa figured there would be less pages to get through. But Maddie says she didn't know when dad fell asleep. 'My goodness, Maddie is just too good for herself', she thought with a sigh.

Narissa really found it very difficult to understand how someone can be so irresponsible. 'I do this every night, plus feed, bathe and put all the children to bed myself. All he had to do was to put them to sleep. I cooked, fed and bathed them, ready for bed.' She thought what a disappointing ending to my day.

"Oh well, in that case let's not waste time." Narissa had to make a choice.

Maddie read all the pages of the book, Narissa signed her booklet and then she had to go to toilet and felt thirsty. Narissa walked into the kitchen to get a glass of water and she almost blew the roof off. Everything was left as she had left. Lawrence had even added his plate, cups and glasses on the kitchen bench. The pots were sitting on the stove. He had obviously done nothing!

Narissa was feeling tired too. If she had left the kitchen in this state she will have to attend to them in the morning which she didn't want to. For her each day is a new beginning, plus you don't know what changes will take place in the morning, what she will be up against.

Anyway, quick small drink for Maddie and off to bed. Maddie fell asleep quite quickly, much to Narissa's delight.

She took some deep breaths and walked to the kitchen. By the time she finished cleaning up, it was nearly 11 pm. Exhausted from first day of being a student, cleaning, preparing for next day, she made her way into the bedroom. It was dark in the room due to the block out curtains Narissa had put in and Lawrence was fast asleep. She wanted to have a shower but didn't want to wake him up. She tip toed around the bedroom, found her sleeping gear, brushed her teeth got into bed. Lawrence doesn't wake up with noise, once he is asleep he won't wake up till his alarm at 7am.

What a day!

There had to be some changes made to this she thought to

herself. After repeatedly reminding Lawrence of her Wednesday night classes and failure to see any changes, Narissa decided to get a babysitter. To hell with Lawrence and his excuses and money issues. She had to do what she had to do to keep sanity.

*"Loneliness is like a soul suffering from poverty."*

# CHAPTER 8

*"Fathers, be your daughter's 1ˢᵗ love and
she'll never settle for anything less."*

AT EIGHT YEARS of age Maddie saw an advertisement in
the local paper for Karate lessons. She desperately wanted
to join. Narissa made some enquiries and found out that
she had to be accompanied by an adult. Knowing she couldn't
participate, considering that it was at 6pm when she has Max and
Ella to think about. She wasn't allowed to hire a baby sitter or get a
cleaner. What to do?

Finally she had the courage to ask Lawrence if he would like to
do Karate with Maddie. "I think you will both enjoy it."

In fact Maddie asked Lawrence and he thought it was a good idea.

She went down one day, did the registrations and the sizing of the
gear called the Dogi. Few weeks later they went to pick up the gear
and Maddie was really excited. Gleaming with joy she said "dad we
have Karate today. Will you meet me there or will you take me there?"

"Oh I will come home and we will go together." Lawrence
replied.

Maddie was counting days. On the first day of her lesson
Maddie had her dinner and she was ready for her lesson. She waited
and waited. She said "dad is late."

Narissa called Lawrence's phone and he didn't answer. So giving him the benefit of the doubt, she thought he is on his way and cannot get to the phone. Clever little Maddie, had been attending Montessori school and learnt to tell the time on an analogue clock. Lawrence turned up and finally they were on their way.

They both enjoyed the first class. Second week Lawrence decided he was going to get serious about this.

Maddie of course likes to perfect everything she does. She tried to practice with her dad but it didn't go down so well. She tried to tell him the moves and I must say she has a better memory than him. But he won't listen to her. He was over riding Maddie, telling her she was wrong. "Maddie, you are only 8, you can't remember! I am your father and an adult and I know." Of course he was never wrong. He was always right and knew everything. No one else had a say.

Frustrated with that attitude, Maddie left and never to practice with him again.

Lawrence decided to purchase the DVD's that the club was selling. He really degrades people. While purchasing the DVD he said to the lady, "My daughter here is 8 and can't remember all the moves. Therefore, I think it is a good idea for me to buy the DVD for her."

Load of crap! He needed the DVD for himself. But why tell Maddie needs it more than himself. Well, he wants to show himself as a good father by buying the DVD but he also wants people to think he is very clever when he goes to classes after perfecting his art. Why can't he say he wants to buy the DVD because he can't remember the moves? Well, he has to push someone down and Maddie being the oldest child always gets this.

Looks like this will be a nice Saturday morning and I can get a lot of washing done. I am running from upstairs to downstairs getting washing into the washing machine after a lengthy breakfast. I say lengthy because I try to make some nice cooked breakfast with scrambled eggs and toast. Ella doesn't like scrambled eggs so I made her eggs and soldiers. The children and I wake up early. I am usually up and see what the weather is doing before deciding to wash clothes or change sheets. Max is 6 now and he can dress himself. He will brush his hair and I have to help him make his bed. Ella usually dresses herself too. She is 4 and tries to make her bed. I must say my children are responsible and would help when they can or asked.

Lawrence always sleeps in till about ten or eleven. He doesn't like it when kids come into our bed in the morning. He will scream at them "I need my sleep, go away!"

I don't like this at all. I think as a parent we have responsibility to our children and we have to give them comfort, nurture them and most of all love them unconditionally.

I am putting the last lot of washing on the line when I hear Maddie screaming. I ran up to the lounge to see what all the commotion is about. She sounded like she was being hurt. "What is happening? Is everyone OK?"

"I hate dad!"

"Maddie, what is it?" "He won't let me watch the Karate DVD." "Why?"

"Dad said he is going to have breakfast first."

OMG! Can he not let her watch the DVD while he is having breakfast? Oh I forgot, he has to be the first one.

If he buys something, he has to be the first one to open it and try it. Nobody has the right to his property. Well, considering he told the lady at the club that his daughter needs to see it and then stopping her from seeing it before himself. That's not the only problem. He snatched it from Maddie's hand because she had a bleeding finger. When I asked her she said "dad snatched the DVD from my hand it hurt." So where is this DVD? He put it high up on the bookshelf so no one could get it. Maddie was crying because there was blood on her finger and he is standing there telling her that she should have listened.

Is it necessary to snatch it off her hands and then try to put it where she can't reach? Is it necessary to stand over a child with a bleeding finger and telling them that it is their fault? "I am not getting a plaster for you because you cut it yourself."

I find that gut wrenching. Anyway, I put a plaster on Maddie's finger and he doesn't stop there. He says "she will remember for the rest of her life to listen."

Well, I think she won't understand why she wasn't allowed to watch a DVD without her father. She will remember how her father hurt her because she didn't understand his reasons.

Can't he just ask "shall we watch together?" No he was never taught how to speak nicely.

'Anyway, I became mean and said sorry, Maddie can watch if she wants to. You can join in after your breakfast.'

It was already 11.45 and it will be time for kid's lunch soon. Narissa knew exactly what will happen. This is normal for Lawrence taking an hour to have his breakfast and then when he is ready, he will want everyone to join him. What he doesn't care is that other people have things to do too. Things cannot happen on his time.

When he is ready Maddie might be having lunch and then he will turn around and say well your fault for not being there. This is a usual Narcissistic behaviour.

So she explained that if Maddie makes a start and you can see the DVD from your dining table, then when you finish you can join her. I am going to prepare lunch and then Maddie can have a break. "But I am full, I just had breakfast."

Is it always just about you? No one is asking you to eat. Does he think if his stomach is full then no one else needs to eat?

The kids have been up since 7.30 this morning. They had breakfast at 8am. Then they played outside. They had a light morning tea with fruits and yoghurt. By 1pm they will need lunch. For heaven's sakes, when will he grow up?

Anyway, Maddie is watching and now Max decides to watch. Maddie watches the introduction and says it is very boring, basically telling them how to prepare for the lesson and she says "we already know all this." I guess the DVD is for people who want to practice at home.

The real bits come on and now everyone is excited. Ella has joined the group. "Dad, look at this?"

Max is having a bit of fun and doing some of the moves. "Dad, are you coming?" Max says excitedly.

"Maddie! I am eating! Leave me alone!" Lawrence speaks with so much vengeance. What a rude man.

"Control your kids!" he shouts out loud angrily to Narissa.

Narissa couldn't care less because by now she had realised that the only way to deal with it is to ignore him.

Almost an hour has passed and Lawrence has just finished eating. He was reading the paper and then while eating his breakfast he was on his phone. As usual, Lawrence takes the dishes to the kitchen and leaves them there. Lawrence comes into the lounge and Maddie says we can rewind. So now he wants to watch all the boring bits. Why waste time?

"Dad look at this move. See, I was right about this one. You have to move from left to right and then punch."

"Well that's what I was saying." Lawrence relies sarcastically.

"No Dad, you were saying it is like this," Maddie is showing Lawrence the moves.

Lucky I had been watching them and I know for a fact he is wrong. He was telling her the other way. What I figured was when he is watching someone he gets confused with left and right. He cannot get coordinated but won't admit it. He will take it as defeat. No one else can be smarter than me, that's Lawrence's attitude.

All the arguments, is it always necessary? The answer is no, but with Lawrence there always has to be a winner, someone has to be right and it is always him.

As the weeks go by he is getting home later and later especially on the days of the karate lesson. So a few times I have had to get all 3 children in the car and get Maddie into the class but she doesn't have a partner to aspire with and she has to be partnered with the teacher, which Maddie doesn't like as she gets a bit shy because everyone is watching her. She didn't used to be so shy, but being told so many times by her dad that she is wrong, she starts doubting her own self.

Maddie was a very confident child, made friends easily, was a real chatter box and extremely caring.

For some reason Lawrence always made Maddie feel like she was useless and couldn't do anything by herself. Lawrence would never say "yes" the first time. If Maddie asked for something, the answer was always "no" and if Maddie insisted then there will be an argument and usually Maddie getting a smack, ears clipped or arms twisted.

Lawrence had to be reminded that he was to think before answering.

Then as the weeks went by, Maddie is getting frustrated because Lawrence is running late very week and only on Monday. Maddie used to have dinner early, get changed and do her homework while waiting for her dad to arrive. Then one day I got a call ten minutes before her lesson to say he will be late again. That day Maddie decided that she won't put up with that crap any more. She was mad. "It is not fair!" "He is late every week and I have to aspire with the teacher. Why can't he tell us earlier that he is going to be late?"

True Maddie, he should organise himself better. 'He has no right to cause stress on an 8 year old like this'. Narissa thought to herself.

Maddie got to yellow belt and was pleased with herself. Lawrence didn't get to the next level as he had missed a lot of the classes and this meant Maddie was better than him which is not the way Lawrence likes. So one day out of the blue he just told Maddie that the lessons were costing too much money and it had to stop. Maddie was not happy but accepted because it was getting too much for her to handle all the arguments with Lawrence.

Same thing happened when the family went fishing one day. Lawrence had to be encouraged a lot to get out and do things. Lawrence had told Narissa how he loved fishing and thought it was a great idea for kids to go fishing with Lawrence, but of course Lawrence needs someone to hold his hand, so despite her busy schedule Narissa decided that she would go with the family. Thinking of going on a fishing trip or doing anything with the children didn't come naturally with Lawrence.

Maddie and Max were very excited while Ella didn't seem to care. Lawrence expected Maddie to know everything and was getting furious for her lack of knowledge in fishing.

"Lawrence, Maddie has never been fishing before and surely you can teach her." Narissa gently patted him on his shoulder and whispered.

"Don't hit me!" Lawrence shrieks out.

Narissa taken aback moved back quietly. Just from past experience she had seen Lawrence over react or misread situations, realising that disagreements with him is not a done thing and justifying herself creates unnecessary arguments, she let it be.

Just ten minutes into fishing, Maddie catches a big snapper. She cannot believe it and neither can anyone else. Lawrence gives a quick glance with eyes saying 'how can she', except he doesn't say a word. Maddie is over the moon and she is jumping with joy on the jetty with her fish hanging by the hook at the end of the rod. "Put it down!" Screamed Lawrence.

"Ella, look at my fish!" Maddie's excitement is too much for Lawrence and too stinky for Ella, who is running away from it all. Max is very interested and tries to grab the rod. Lawrence had no interest in Maddie's catch. Reluctantly, Narissa grabbed Maddie's rod but didn't have a clue as to what to do. Lawrence threw a glance and stood up. She saw him approaching angrily towards them. Narissa had already preparing scenarios her my head. What's he going to do?

Lawrence grabbed the rod angrily out of her hands, pushed Maddie to the side "you guys are so loud, embarrassing and look at you all! Never seen a fish on a hook before?"

"I was about to get the hook off." Narissa replied quietly.

He looks at Maddie, "so now you think you are too smart, catching a fish. When I was your age I used to catch really huge fish and lots of them. Let's see how many you catch. Beat that, huh!" Lawrence tells Maddie and stomps off.

Unbelievable!

Maddie has a battle on her hands with a father who has this sort of attitude. Narissa is gobsmacked. She told herself, 'we will never go fishing again, not with Lawrence.'

The fish off the hook and Maddie wants to cast out again. Lawrence won't prepare her rod. He sat with his own one stubbornly. She can't stand the smell or the texture of this bait which she thinks is squid. Somehow Narissa managed to get the bait on the hook and cast it out for Maddie. It didn't go out too far out but not bad.

"Oh no mummy, you didn't get it far out into the sea!" Maddie is jumping on the jetty.

"I know. Let's just see what happens." Narissa said assuring.

Gosh Maddie managed to catch 2 more fishes and they were small Herrings but she was happy.

An hour had gone past and Lawrence was sitting with his rod as if he was ready to kill someone.

Max comes running down the jetty and saw the fishes in the bucket. "Dad! Dad! Maddie has caught 3 fishes."

Lawrence is not interested.

"Honey, you want to see what Maddie has caught?" Narissa called out empathetically.

Lawrence ignored it and Narissa pretended that he didn't hear them.

Another hour later, Maddie had caught some small blow fishes and which had to be thrown out. Maddie being Maddie kept the number of fishes she had caught in her head. There were 3 in the bucket and 4 she had thrown out, altogether she had caught 7 fishes. Max had a go of throwing the rod out which looked really dangerous. Narissa thought he was going to fly off with the rod. With a bit of help, they managed to cast out. Max didn't have the patience so ran off to play with Ella on the rocks.

"Dad, I caught 7 fishes today." Maddie is so happy. She is skipping and jumping with joy.

"What are you trying to say, that I haven't caught anything?" Lawrence is looking at everyone with frustration.

Shabina

"Honey, that's not what Maddie is saying. She is so proud of her catch. For someone who hasn't done any fishing before, isn't that a great result?" I felt that Lawrence had misunderstood Maddie.

"We need to move from here. It is not good." Lawrence starts packing up.

"Where do you want to go?" I am looking around to see where other people are fishing.

"Well, I used to catch a lot of fish but you guys are very noisy." Lawrence tells everyone.

"I am sorry honey, kids are just kids." Narissa replied, gently patting the kids on their backs.

"Where's Max? Being a boy he should be out here helping me." Shrieks Lawrence.

They had to pack everything up and get into the car with Lawrence driving around and around looking for a good spot.

"I want to go home now." Ella can't hold it any more. She hates the smell of fish and the sea air.

"Shut up, Ella. I am looking for a place to fish." Lawrence shrieks angrily and is determined to catch something today.

It is not all evident whether he wants to outdo Maddie or he is jealous that she has caught something and he hasn't. If he loved his children he would have called it quits and taken them all home and come back another time. Not Lawrence, he will carry on his mission till he gets what his way and in the meantime no one else matters.

Finally, they found a place that Lawrence thought was a good fishing spot. He took his tackle box, bait and rod and off he went. The children were all tired by the look of things. Max was bored and so was Ella. Maddie started playing on the rocks. Narissa nor the kids wanted to continue with this fishing expedition but had no choice. If she dares asking Lawrence to go home, he will bark down her throat as if she was the meanest person on earth. What he failed to see is that kids were tired, and they can only stay out for a few hours not a whole day.

"So you think you are very smart, catching fish, huh Maddie?" Lawrence asks Maddie as she was approaching him.

What a thing to say. I don't think Maddie even thought that way.

"Lawrence, we really need to get going. The sun has gone down and it is getting cold. Both Ella and Max need to rest now. I need to get home and get dinner organised as well." Narissa was getting concerned.

"This is the best time to fish. I am getting something." Lawrence replies like a little boy.

"Lawrence, think about the children. This is their first fishing trip and don't make it their last. You want them to enjoy the trip and not have bad memories." I don't want to sound like I am his mother but I think I am beginning to sound like one.

The children have had some hot milo from the thermos, crackers and fruit. That is not a substantial meal. Narissa can't get Lawrence to move.

She can't leave him and come back because the children might fall asleep after a day out at the beach and then how will she drive back to pick up Lawrence.

Two hours later, Lawrence caught a fish. Surely he should be happy to have caught one. Max comes running out of the car, excited when he saw Lawrence pulling his rod in. "Dad, your fish is smaller than Maddie's." Max just gives it as is. Kids just say what comes to them.

Maddie examines her fish and sure enough, she caught a bigger one than Lawrence.

He is offended. "So you all think Maddie is a fisherman now, do you?"

Lawrence is competing with his daughter who is 8? Really?

"Happy, you caught one. Now let's go home, please. I have so much to do at home." Narissa is pleading with Lawrence.

Since he won't listen, she started packing everything up.

"What are you doing, bitch!" Lawrence exclaims.

"What the hell! Did I hear that right? Kids are all around us so she just pretend that she didn't hear that."

Lawrence was forced to call it a day. He moaned all the way home that he was getting bites and would have caught more had we stayed longer. They had been out for 5 hours and that is more than the kids can handle.

Getting home, listening to his crap was making Narissa nauseous, plus the smell of bait was not very pleasant either. 'Never again! We won't be fishing ever again!' she thought.

Arriving home was no fun either. Lawrence just left for the bathroom, leaving everything as is in the garage and the laundry. Narissa got the kids in the shower and they were all hungry. She decided on a quick simple dinner today as it was getting late. It was very dark outside now. They should have got some takeaways considering how late it was. According to Lawrence, they can't do that because eating takeaways costs a lot of money especially with the kids and yet he eats out every day. So Narissa compromises and quickly cooked eggs on baked beans and toast. There must be left overs in the fridge that they can have. At this stage she was expecting some help from Lawrence, yet knowing that it was a very unlikely scenario.

"Breakfast at dinner?" exclaimed Maddie.

Cooking, feeding, putting kids to bed, cleaning afterwards is all Narissa's responsibility, because according to Lawrence that's what a woman's role is.

Lawrence walks into the kitchen expecting food prepared as if someone was cooking for him. "What are we having, because I haven't eaten all day?" very abruptly he announces.

"You can cook whatever you want. There is some left over in the fridge. I don't have much time as kids need to get to bed." Narissa hurriedly told him and left.

"They can go to bed themselves." Lawrence is always stern when he speaks with family.

"Sure can but I still have to get them moving." Narissa told him.

"Muum, I am thirsty," Maddie comes out with Max behind her.

"You bastards! I have spent entire afternoon with you all! No attention seeking here! Get to bed at once! I mean right now!!" Lawrence looks scary.

He must be tired himself.

Ella is out "Mumma, I feel sick."

"Maddie darling, if you drink water now you will want to pee in the middle of the night." I am trying to diffuse the toxic atmosphere here.

How about I make you all a warm milk drink. This usually puts everyone to bed and also it is nourishing. The sea air for 5 hours at this stage obviously has thrown everyone off their kilter.

"Lawrence, please have your dinner. Don't wait for me." I am ever so kind and sympathetic. I feel Lawrence is tired and wind battered but he won't say it.

"What's there to eat?" Lawrence walks around the kitchen looking useless.

'I have always known one little fact. Lawrence hates it when I attend to children over him.' Narissa thinks to herself. He acts incompetent. He calls Narissa names and tells her that she is the root course of arguments in the family, that she should pay attention to his needs and he comes first. He is the father and that means he is the number one.

Well hello, welcome to the 20th century.

Warm milk drinks with a hint of nutmeg and ginger will surely get the kids rested. Ella felt better and Maddie and Max were both happy after their drinks. Everyone in bed and after her dinner, washing up and putting towels in the wash, emptying out the picnic basket, Narissa is ready to crash.

Lawrence is watching the News. He makes it sound like it is very important to watch the news. Narissa walked into the lounge and Lawrence looks up "I am just watching the News", as if out of guilt.

Geez, did I even say anything? Thought Narissa.

Shabina

The unbelievable thing is Lawrence has no intention of cleaning up the fishing gear. He is happy to go to bed and falls asleep straight away.

"Parents were the only ones obligated to love you; from the rest of the world you had to earn it."

— <u>Ann Brashares</u>

# CHAPTER 9

*"I gave them life, they give me a reason to live mine."*

"**O**MG! ANOTHER CHANGE of school? I am done with this! I don't care which school the kids go to. They will perform if they are interested. No!" Narissa is trying to tell Lawrence.

Lawrence had to change schools, didn't he? "Private is better", he says.

"I don't see how. If the kids have a great support system at home, they will perform anywhere. Private or public, what does it matter? Local school is good because they will have their friends around them." Narissa is pleading.

He seems to think that higher socio economic groups send their children to private schools. It means higher school fees. 'How the heck are we going to afford that?' thought Narissa.

Narissa herself went to a Private school in her secondary years but that's because her parents had planned for it and saved up for it. Being out of town, her parents wanted the best for her and since Narissa wanted to study in the city, her parents didn't want her to go flatting, and they sent her to a Private all girls' boarding school.

When she married Lawrence she said her children will go to a Private school but that didn't mean she had to stick with it, especially when Lawrence didn't want to save money for it either. Lawrence didn't see the need for saving, investing or having any type of insurances.

Anyway, the school that Lawrence is looking at is at the other end of town and it will take Narissa at least 30min to get there, if not more. Not only that, Ella is still at pre-school and that means driving west.

Without taking into consideration any of Narissa's view, Lawrence went ahead and changed the schools. Maddie and Max will now go to a school south of where they lived. The thought of so much driving was killing Narissa already, especially in the winter months.

The only solution we found was that Lawrence was going to drop Maddie and Max in the morning. Phew!

His workplace being just around the corner from the school meant he was able to drop them off in the morning and the kids start at 8.20am which means he will be at work by 8.30am. The kids will have to be ready by 7.50am latest.

Narissa pondered on it for a while and thought maybe that's not a bad idea because it will give Lawrence an opportunity to connect with the children.

First day of new school, Max is a bit anxious and he is ready way too early. He is rechecking his bag to see that he has everything in it. He is scared that he may not be able to make friends.

Maddie is too excited, maybe it is nerves. Maddie is singing and skipping. She is ready too.

Both kids are ready for school. Lawrence, who is normally gone by eight is not ready. It is 7.45am and now the kids were putting the pressure on him to leave home.

The kids finally got to school but late. Their form time is from 8.20-8.30am, after that they have the chapel service and the classes resume 8.50am.

This saga continued for a whole term. Maddie was mad that she gets to school late every day. The kids refused to go to school with

Lawrence and he didn't work out why. The only thing he comes up with is the kids hate him, kids don't like him.

There was no easy solution but for Narissa to start rethinking the whole arrangement.

She tried to speak with Lawrence and tell him that it was important for the children to be at school on time every day. It's not like they were not ready in the morning.

In the second term there was parent teacher interview arranged. Narissa asked if Lawrence would like to attend. He immediately shut her down.

"I am so busy at work! How can you even suggest that I go to these stupid meetings? They are not that important! It is just a formality. Fucks sakes. I am surprised you have asked me. You so dumb!" He screamed at Narissa.

Obviously Narissa had to go by herself. At the parent teacher interview she was reminded to get the kids to school on time.

The form teacher explained that "It is important that the kids attend form time because that's when all the notices are handed out and it is when kids get to meet each other." Narissa felt like a failed parent. She couldn't say anything to the teachers but look sheepishly down. Maddie's teacher said, "Maddie is late every day and she has told me that the school bus is usually late. Is there anything the school can do to help? We can make a call to the transport department and get that sorted."

Maddie, had clearly lied, because she doesn't catch the bus.

That explained why the kids didn't want to go with their father.

Narissa picked up Max and Maddie from school and thought it was a good idea to talk to them about being late to school. Maddie was the first one to speak out as Max usually seems to be unfazed by all the fuss. Maddie is extremely angry and says "mum, we have told dad so many times that we have to be dropped off by 8.15am as it takes 5 minutes to walk up and get to the classrooms. The teachers are always telling us off and I have to rush to get my books!" I miss form times and it is embarrassing to walk in late.

Narissa turned to Max and he just sat there like he doesn't care. Narissa is not sure whether he is just blocking out what he is experiencing or he is just so fed up that he is totally oblivious to it all.

That night when Lawrence arrived home late around 9pm, Narissa gently approached him about the kids being late to school, which she had only discovered at the parent teacher interview. She asked him if he knew. Initially he totally ignored her, then she asked again and his response baffled Narissa, "you're making a big deal out of something so small."

Huh!

"It is important for children to get to school by 8.20am, the school has said that. The form teacher has told me that Maddie has told her that her bus comes in late. The school is happy to talk to transport company to see what they can do." Narissa explains. In fact Maddie couldn't tell the specific bus number she was travelling on and that made the form teacher think that she was lying.

Lawrence couldn't care less. "Well, they get to school and that's what matters."

"Lawrence, I don't understand you!" Narissa screams out.

Usual Lawrence self, he just plays hard to get and doesn't respond with an adequate explanation. Frustrated, Narissa walks away. She feels helpless when Lawrence does that. He won't respond to her questions, he won't give an honest answer and either acts dumb or just looks down and ignores her. She feels so alone, yet again.

It is Monday morning and Max is refusing to go to school. He is beside himself, not wanting to go. "What is it Max? Don't you want to see your friends?" Narissa asks.

"I don't want to be late again!" he replied angrily.

Well, Narissa was not going to argue. So she had to pack Max and the girls and they just took off driving down the hill, through the city, the traffic was quite heavy and Narissa was losing her patience. She kept a close eye on the clock and thinking what was she doing.

They made it through the heavy traffic and it is 8.15am. The kids were happy because they have spotted their friends and couldn't wait to get out of the car to join them. Narissa drove into kiss and drive and Max hopped out even before Narissa brought the car to a complete halt. She saw the look on Maddie's face, so happy. She threw a kiss at Narissa and hopped off the car before her friends took off. She joined them and turned around to say "I love you mumma. See you later Ella."

Narissa could see how happy the kids were walking together with their friends. He has this glee on his face that reminded Narissa of when she baked him the Thomas the Tank Engine cake for his 5th Birthday. He was over the moon then.

Narissa had used her imagination and baked 2 rectangle cakes, cut them up, used icing, lollies, cookies and chocolate buttons and made train on a track. She was very impressed with herself.

That's the look she got from Max and she knew they will all have a great day at school today.

Now she has to drive back through the city, up the hill and drop Ella at 9am at her pre-school. If she has to do this every day, then Ella will have to be woken up earlier and driven around for an hour before being dropped off to her pre-school. Poor Ella.

After school Narissa drove down to pick the kids up and they were so happy. Both Max and Maddie had storied to tell and Max said "for once we were on time mum. Good job! I love you."

It just melted Narissa's heart. Happy kids, happy home.

That night after dinner she asked Lawrence again, if he could take the kids in the morning but they had to leave home by 7.50 the latest, she said.

Tuesday morning, Maddie was ok going with Lawrence but Max wasn't. He told Lawrence that mum had taken them to school on time and he didn't want that ruined because no one told him off for being late and he didn't get laughed at by other kids. This made Narissa think if there were bullying issues at school. She decided to let it go because she didn't want to put ideas in the kids' head which could become a bigger deal than it was.

On hearing that Lawrence just took off. He didn't want Max to talk to him like that. Narissa had no choice but to get them all in the car and drive off speedily to get them to school. After 3 more terms, she was feeling it. Narissa had back issues and the point where she had the epidural stuck in while delivering Maddie was absolutely painful. Ella was also grumpy some days and they had to start their journey earlier in case Ella didn't corporate.

The year was over and Narissa felt like she was the taxi driver. While Lawrence enjoyed his morning breakfasts with work colleagues and had a free run to work, Narissa had the tough time going through the day with extra driving. She never looked back, she just got on with her commitment.

Before the start of the New Year she approached Lawrence to see perhaps they could move Ella to the pre-school at the same school as Maddie and Max.

"I am not made of money!" Shrieked Lawrence.

"Then how am I supposed to do this on my own?" shrieked Narissa.

For whole 2 years, she had to drive back and forth, till Ella started school. Lawrence just plainly refused to take the children to school on time.

'Children are the anchors that hold a mother to life.' Sophocles

# CHAPTER 10

*"Time spent playing with children is never wasted"* – Dawn Lentero

WHEN MAX WAS 3, he really wanted a sand pit. In fact Maddie wanted one when she was 3 as well. Narissa couldn't convince Lawrence to buy one and she didn't put unnecessary pressure on Lawrence due to financial stress. Their good old neighbour decided to throw her one out as her boys had outgrown theirs. Narissa quickly grabbed it and then spent a few days bringing sand across over the fence. Of course both Colin and Gary gave her a hand with that. It took Lawrence 2 weeks to realise that they had a sand pit in the backyard. He was furious. He asked Narissa why he wasn't informed and he was extremely upset with the sandpit. Narissa asked him several times the reasons for not wanting it but got nothing, no explanations whatsoever. She thought maybe he didn't want a second hand one or maybe he wasn't part of the process, objects for the sake of it because it wasn't his choice.

Both Maddie and Max spent a lot of time in the sandpit.

Then one day while she was out doing the grocery shopping with the children she came find the sand pit gone. Both Maddie and Max were furious.

Narissa asked Lawrence about it and he just shrugged his

shoulders, head down as usual and not a single word. "Why did you throw it out?" she asked again and again and getting angry.

"It was old and tatty. I am going to get a better one." Lawrence says it as if he really means that.

Of course it didn't happen for almost another six months.

Max couldn't play with his diggers in the back yard and Maddie loved playing with her sand castle building toys which she got for Christmas from her grandparents. She was furious.

Narissa knew the kids were missing it but she just let it be. She had given up on Lawrence's promises as well. At first he said he was going to make one but when he was out at the hardware shops they didn't have all the material. Then another time he snapped out and said that he didn't want a sand pit at home because kids will bring sand in the house. Narissa couldn't understand his unreasonable explanations and had never been able to understand Lawrence's excuses.

Max got given a lot of Bob the builder toys for his birthday and he wanted to play in a sandpit. With Lawrence, you have to make everything sound like it is important to have, for example the sand pit is great for hand eye coordination and it helps develop motor skills.

While at the local garden centre one day Narissa saw clam shells with a cover, ideal for a sand pit or paddling pool for $15.00. Unable to resist it she bought it. With Max's help they both tried to fit it in the back of the car. With the helping hand from a young assistant they were able to get it into the car. Narissa could see Max getting really excited. His eyes were full of happiness but what he didn't realise was that they didn't have any sand to put in. She had asked the garden centre staff and they directed her to the other hardware stores.

Saturday mornings Lawrence disappears and Narissa thought that he was either going to Bunnings or Mitre 10 or Placemakers or somewhere for coffee, but she had no idea. Narissa never questioned his whereabouts just so to avoid the put downs. On the other hand if she went out without any explanation, Lawrence gets into full fledge anger.

"Honey, if you happen to go past Bunnings or somewhere like that, could you see if they have sand for sand pits?" Narissa asked Lawrence as he was about to leave on a Saturday afternoon.

No reply.

Few hours later Lawrence arrived and she asked him if he managed to look for sand for the sand pit. "No one has them." he snapped.

"See you shouldn't have got that big crap!" he carried on.

'Oh shit', Narissa thought to herself. What was she going to do?

Every weekend for a few weeks Lawrence would come home and say "that stupid sand pit is an eye sore. No one has the sand. I will take it to the tip."

'Seriously, is he trying to emotionally hurt us?' thought Narissa.

Max asked her a few times if dad would bring the sand. "Max, honey dad hasn't found any yet. I am sure he will."

"You are lying, Mum!" exclaimed Maddie. Maddie hears everything, I don't know how. She is so switched on. "Dad said he is taking it to the tip! I heard him."

"You are lying, Mum." Snarled Maddie.

"Oh Maddie, dad doesn't mean that." I said caressing her shoulders and stooping down to hug her. She pushed me away. Maddie is angry. "Max has wanted a sand pit for a long time. I wanted one too but dad said he didn't want one."

"Maddie, I am so sorry you feel this way. We will get some sand, OK."

"Why don't we fill this sand pit with water and bring the bath toys out?" Narissa said eagerly with a sudden brilliant idea that sprung to herb mind.

Both Maddie and Max jumped with joy. "Yay!"

"Let's do that!" Maddie is happy again. I love seeing the children smile and be happy. Kids love the water so it is a win win situation.

Monday morning after dropping the children to school, Narissa detoured to the hardware store and asked for some assistance regarding sand for the sand pit. She was ushered to a different part of the Placemakers store, which is actually the building and construction part. She didn't know how much to get and ended up getting two bags of 25 kg of golden sand for the sand pit.

"Have you just recently got these in?" she asked the assistance.

"Um, nah darl, we have always had them. All the school and pre-schools get it from here but they get the bulk by the scoop from the back." The assistance replied.

"Will the 2 bags be enough for the clam shell, then?" Narissa asked.

"Absolutely. If you need more, we are here. It will always be here." replied the assistance. She knew the clam shell Narissa was talking about. From her description any parent would know what she was talking about.

Narissa realised then that Lawrence had lied to them. She knew he was lying because of the way he had snapped about it every time she asked him and also the desire to throw the brand new sand pit out into the tip made her think of his cunning ways of manipulating situations. Instead of suggesting that they give the sandpit to the neighbours or friends, he just casually suggested that they throw it out. In other words if they didn't have the sand pit then he won't have to continuously lie about the sand.

'Typical Lawrence! What a carniving cruel person he has turned out to be' thought Narissa.

"Hey darl, hope you have help at the other end when you are unloading them. Promise me that you won't attempt to lift them yourself. They are heavy." Yelled the assistance.

"Thank you, yes I will get hubby to unload." Narissa said with a smile.

She was getting so good at covering her real inner feelings. She knew that Lawrence wouldn't help out but Narissa was always hopeful and remained positive.

She went home and tried to lift the sand bag and it wouldn't budge. 'Bloody hell! This lady was right. The sand is sitting in the boot of her Honda odyssey 4WD and she can't move it, not even an inch. Thoughts rushing through her head right now. 'I will just say to Lawrence that I managed to get some sand and if he could help me carry it to the sand pit will be great.' That won't work.

"Honey, guess what? I managed to get some sand today. It is too heavy for me to carry the bags to the back of the house. Do you have time to help me carry them to the back?" Narissa is just rehearsing in her head all the different ways to approach Lawrence.

This is what it takes to approach a Narcissistic. I have to suss what mood he is in and what words to use and what tones to use, every single time she needs to ask him to do something.

It is nearly 9pm and Lawrence has just arrived home from work. Narissa was exhausted but she was willing to see if he was approachable. At dinner table, Narissa brought it up after listening to his rant about work which she has to do every day. Lawrence needs to off load to someone every day. Maybe he wants Narissa to think he has a tough life out at work. If Narissa doesn't listen then he bullies her into thinking that she is a bad wife, she doesn't care and blah blah. Lawrence never says anything good about people at his work. He is always telling her all the bad things and how bad people are. Sometimes she wonders how he goes to work every day and spends entire day with people he can't stand.

"Oh guess what? I managed to get some sand for the sand pit. Isn't that great?" Narissa tells him raising her head and voice in excitement splashing the words out.

"Only thing is I can't lift it out of the car." she says it casually and laughingly. "The bags are really heavy. Shall we move them tonight?" she asked politely.

"Why did you buy it if it is heavy? Can't do it tonight." Lawrence answers abruptly.

Why did I buy it if it is heavy? Is that a valid question? I wonder about this guy.

"Well, I have had it for 2 days in the car now." I paused to see his reaction. "I couldn't ask you last 2 days because you were very busy."

Lawrence is always busy.

She couldn't say much more so she left it.

Next morning the kids found the sand bags in the boot of the car and couldn't wait to get it all set up. Narissa promised them they will get it out and set up the sand pit soon. So after dropping the children to school she came home and tried to lift the bags again one more time. She was heaving, pulling, pushing and trying to lift with a spade as a crane and just then she heard a voice behind her "don't pick that up!" Tom runs from across the road yelling. "This isn't a job for a girl! This is too heavy for a girl. Get Lawrence to do this!"

"I have been asking Lawrence for the last 3 days and he won't. Unfortunately, the kids have found it so I have to make an effort." Narissa said in a laughing voice.

Tom picked up the bag and swayed it around over on his shoulders and carried them up the slope to the back of the house to the sandpit. He came back and took the other one. "Pass me a cutter, and I can get your sandpit filled up. The kids will be very happy with you today." Tom smiles. He is Scandinavian with a beautiful tanned body and blonde hair.

"I can't thank you enough Tom. Thank you so much. I really appreciate your help." Narissa was so humbled.

"Don't ever try doing stuff like this." Tom says angrily his eyes fixated on Narissa with raised eyebrows, but in a caring angry way.

"You know what Lawrence is like." She said. "It is very difficult to get him to do anything. We have waited 3 months for the sand. Now that I have finally got it, I can't get Lawrence to set it up for the kids. He is just too busy."

Narissa picked the kids from school and Maddie immediately looked in the boot of the car, "mum, where is the sand?"

She doesn't miss anything, this Maddie of hers.

"In the sandpit? I hope." Maddie is smiling with that hopeful look on her face.

"Oh Max, we can play in the sand pit today!" Exclaimed Maddie.

"Yippee!" exclaimed Ella.

The first thing Max did as soon as they reached home, he

grabbed all his Bob the builder toys and ran for the sandpit. Maddie is already there screaming with joy and Ella is right there with her beach toys, a little hand spade and a bucket. The happiness on the children's faces is something Narissa likes to see every day. It is priceless. It makes her feel so worthy and fulfilled that she couldn't give this up for the world. 'Why would I ever want to change that?'

'How can Lawrence deprive the children of this kind of happiness?' she thought.

Lawrence is not a happy man and Narissa has just figured it out. His father didn't pay him attention as a child but Narissa would have thought that Lawrence would be more than happy to spend time with his own children. Perhaps she was wrong. Perhaps he doesn't know how to. At least given all the opportunities, she thought he might just get involved.

Lawrence can be very insensitive. He doesn't understand what an inner happiness means. He doesn't understand how little things like getting sand in the sand pit can create such an amazing happiness for a child.

His mother and sisters gave him far too much attention and gave in to his demands and that's why he has developed this Narcissistic personality.

Max was most unhappy one day when Lawrence decided to play with his remote controlled car, which Narissa had purchased on- line for his 10th birthday. She had spoken to a representative over the phone and it seemed like the right toy for Max, who absolutely adored his car, which was like a real car with gear changing noises, a petrol tank and a small set of tools to change tyres and fiddle with the engine parts. Max played with his car almost every day after school. As soon as the car stopped in the garage, Max would get his seatbelt off, push open the door and run to grab his car from the shelf in the garage. He would check the petrol and if it was empty, he would get the funnel and fill it up. Narissa always supervised this because she didn't like Max to fill up petrol himself.

The strict instructions were to drive the car on driveways, concrete paths but not on dirt or sand because it could break the clutch.

Lawrence decided to play with it one Saturday morning. Max heard the car engine and ran to see who was playing with his car. "Dad! What are you doing?" To be honest, Lawrence had never bought anything for the kids and Max was not happy. "Dad! You are not to drive on the dirt!"

Why would Lawrence pay any attention?

"D-ad! The dirt will cause the clutch to break! You are meant to drive it on the path and concrete only."

Lawrence wouldn't give a damn what Max was saying. He continued pushing the car up on the mountain of dirt and playing is ruggedly. Max ran to grab the car but before he could get there the car stopped with a thud and wouldn't move.

Max picked it up and realised that his toy was probably broken now.

"It's not a good car. The battery needs changing on the remote." Lawrence is looking down at the remote. He has no idea what this car is about and continues as if he is the boss and knows it all. Max picked up the car and brought it over. He took his tools out to open the engine.

"Stop, stop, what are you doing!" Lawrence exclaims at Max.

Max left the car and went to see Narissa.

"Mum, my car broke." The look on his face was very sad. "Mum, I didn't break it, I swear. Dad drove it on the neighbours dirt pile and I told him not to. He just wouldn't listen, mum". Max is in tears.

"Here, come here. Give me a hug." Narissa knelt down to hug Max.

He had tears in his eyes and with pouty lips, he angrily burst out "I hate dad."

Then on top of his head "I h-ate Dad."

"Max, you don't mean that. I am sure daddy can fix that for you." Narissa calmly tells Max while hugging him and caressing his head.

"No, he won't. Like everything else he breaks. It isn't his, is it? He doesn't care." Max is getting a bit angry.

"Have you forgotten my helicopter? He broke that too and he blamed me for it." Max explains.

In fact Narissa had bought the remote control helicopter for Max' for Christmas and they used to go down to the park to fly. The remote control had a charging unit but Lawrence had thrown the cord out and then to make things worse he flew the helicopter in their small back yard and crashed it on a hard stone. The worst part is Lawrence laughed when it broke and also made it look like it was nothing, it was just a small toy bound to be broken. In fact Max had played with his helicopter for almost a year.

Narissa remembered that day and hated how Lawrence just laughed at the broken helicopter. So she could really understand how Max was feeling right now.

"I will get Daddy to fix it, okay?" She looked at Max in the eye and helped him straighten up and be strong.

Narissa went into the garage and explained to Lawrence what the car meant to Max and how he was feeling right now.

Lawrence just shrugged his shoulders and went "oh well. It was just a toy, no big deal. I can get a better one than that"

"Lawrence, to Max it is a big deal. It was a good car for his age. He looked forward to coming home after school and playing with his car. Why couldn't you listen to him when he said don't take it into the dirt?" Narissa's anger is rising with Lawrence's lack of empathy.

"You broke it you fix it." She stormed out.

On Monday morning Narissa called the company where she bought the car from. They said the clutch needed to be repaired and it was $70 for replacement. The part had to be ordered from a different state.

Narissa related this message to Lawrence and he just casually buffed her off.

"You said yesterday that you will fix it! It is not a big deal! What has happened now?" She shrieked.

"Well, I can't afford $70." Lawrence replied.

"You can't afford $70 and yet you could afford to break it!" Narissa shrieked again.

"I didn't know." Lawrence replied. "It isn't my fault."

"Hold it. Max told you not to take the car on the dirt pile and you deliberately took it on it not once, but several times, ignoring his pleas. You break it and now you refuse to fix it?" Narissa is shouting at Lawrence full throttle.

"How is this not YOUR fault?" She wanted to know what Lawrence was thinking.

She knew that because it was a toy that her and Max had bought, Max loved it and was always involved with it, Lawrence was jealous. He can never see anyone happy.

Lawrence was checking the bank account to make sure Narissa hadn't purchased the clutch. Narissa couldn't anyway because he had changed the account details and she didn't know how to make purchases on line any more.

"It wasn't the best toy anyway." Lawrence replied with a smirk on his face.

Narissa felt like clawing his face but she walked away knowing it was a waste of time to argue with this dickhead.

Max was really mad and didn't want to know about the car any more.

"Parents do not have the right to hurt their children" —Ingrid Holm-Garibay

# CHAPTER 11

*"Men are supposed and love and respect their wives,*
*not to hurt and betray them" –Anon.*

KIDS HAVE BEEN going to this school for 3 years now. They are all happy because they get to school on time, have more friends now and are doing really well. Now they are confident enough to catch the school bus home. Narissa drives down to the shops where the bus drops them off after school. The danger in that is if she is a bit late they go to the deli to buy lollies. Max buys for the shapes, Ella loves colours and Maddie just buys for the size, the bigger the better. None of them like the lollies as much and Narissa finds them stuck to the car seat belt, right at the bottom inside the school bag sometimes stuck outside the bag or in their room under the bed.

Today, she had the flu and couldn't drive the children to the school. She asked Lawrence if he could help out. He just replied 'no', he has meetings today. His meeting is at 10, because Narissa heard him over the phone talking to someone saying he will be there by 9 for a coffee as he has a meeting at 10 not far from his favourite coffee shop.

The kids are all sad for their mum because Narissa feels really cold, her limbs all ache and she had a terrible headache. She felt tired and was shivering. Max is happy to miss school. Ella is not bothered either way but Maddie is unhappy about missing school. So how does Narissa do this? All the kids in the neighbourhood go to the two local primary schools. No one will be able to take 3 kids down across town to the other side for school.

She asked Lawrence again if he could drop them by 8.20am as she was not able to. He will have enough time to meet his mate for coffee at 9. Max is very vocal these days, "Dad, you are very selfish. Did you know that school starts at 8.20?"

"No, no-one told me." That is such bullshit! "It says in our school diary too."

"I want to stay at home with mum. You can drop the girls to school."

Maddie comes into the room, "dad can you please take us now! I can't be late and you can change your coffee meeting, can't you?"

Of course Maddie doesn't understand that he won't change his engagements for anyone except his own family. Who could Narissa call on? Her mum and dad were 40 minutes away and then the traffic situation. They were retired and Narissa couldn't put them out like this.

Maddie was getting very anxious and Narissa could see that she was ready to explode. She is 12 now and she is at that stage when once a month her reaction to any discomfort is just a tad over the top.

Narissa got out of bed, feeling dizzy. She took some medications but felt really sick in her stomach. She tried to pick herself up and get some strength and she was slouching dragging herself to the bathroom. She couldn't see herself behind the wheels and didn't want to be a danger to herself, my children nor other drivers on the road.

As she sat on the cold toilet seat, shivering like a soft leaf being pelted with rain, her brain suddenly fired and she thought Maddie and Ella might have to go in a cab. If they want to be on time, she had to call the cab now.

By now Maddie is feeling helpless and Narissa can hear her shrieking. She can almost hear her being slapped because she is screaming. She is helpless, she can't be late to school and yet she cannot get there herself.

Narissa pulled herself out of the bathroom, slowly stammered across the room to get into bed. She stooped like a hunch back and was tagging at the sheet to get in. Barely made it into her bed when the voice came from behind.

"Oh you are up, you can take the kids. I can go now." No that was not a question, it was statement from Lawrence.

'How insensitive is he? Can he not see my state? My heart is beginning to bleed now. I can feel my heart pumping that extra blood, my body is giving off heat not just from the flu but from anger. I feel dizzy just looking at him with droopy eyes, throbbing headache and stomach that feels like there is something huge brewing inside, ready to erupt out of belly button if it could. I am feeling heavy, lethargic. Honestly, does he think I am faking it? He hasn't taken my temperature or even looked at me. The kids could tell I was unwell.' Narissa is in tears.

"Are you able to take the girls, please?" Now she is begging him.

"I told you I have meetings." He replied.

'How do I tell him I have overheard him on his mobile? If I do then I am eves dropping, which I have been accused of before. Like that time he offered to fix someone's computer and I overheard. I butted in and said we had plans for Saturday, which we did and he had forgotten. We had to look at some furniture and then visit a friend in the afternoon. He told me off in the car because he said looking at furniture was not important and visiting the friend could have been changed to another time. Always everyone else before family.'

Lawrence just took off, leaving Narissa on her own.

Cab it is she thought. She quickly called the cab and found out how long it will take them to arrive and get the girls to school. The cab arrived pretty fast and got the girls to school on time. They were happy to be on time but Narissa was worried.

The conversation came up one day that taxi service was used and $35.00 came out of the credit card account.

"Surely you remember the day I had the flu and you refused to take the kids to school because you had a coffee meeting at 9?" Oops the coffee meeting slipped out of Narissa's lips. He was not to know that she knew he had a coffee meeting.

"That was an important meeting." Lawrence replies and Narissa can always tell when he is lying.

Mind you is there any meeting that is not important for him? He was just catching up with a friend, she knew it and he knew it. Narissa was getting sick of all his lies.

The conversation went on and on him trying to tell her that if she took the kids to school on the day she had the flu, they would be $35 better off. Narissa was made to feel guilty for bringing on the flu. She was made to feel that she overspent on an unnecessary item.

He had done nothing wrong! She did all the wrong.

Would he call the school to say kids were not coming to school? Would he stay home to mind the children? The answer is 'NO'.

Narissa didn't tell him that kids had to be dropped off before 8.20am Lies, lies and more lies.

*"If you fight back and get hit, it hurts a little while; if you don't fight back it hurts forever."* Joel Siegel

# CHAPTER 12

*"You didn't just cheat on me; you cheated on us. You didn't just break my heart; you broke our future."* —Steve Maraboli

NARISSA HAD BEEN getting friend requests from Friendstar and Facebook but she wasn't allowed to use the computer much. They had an old PC, with a hard drive and few disks that she had some material stored on. The internet service at home was shocking. Even her retired parents had a better computer and internet service. Most of Narissa's friends have internet and chat on social media sites and share pictures.

Lawrence told Narissa that these sites were not secure and not to use them because they were very dangerous.

'What does he think of me? An uneducated bimbo that she will post objectionable material and embarrass herself? I don't know what he thinks.'

One thing is for sure, if Lawrence doesn't have something then no one else can. If he doesn't know about something then no one else can either.

People had requested so many times for Narissa to go on social media site like Facebook or Linkedin. She had heard that there are some really good educational material on facebook and also

Linkedin which is more for professional people, where you can find jobs and interact with people of the same calibre.

Unbeknown to Lawrence, Narissa did the unthinkable. One day she opened up her email and received a friend request on facebook. She accepted this invitation from an old friend in USA. She has joined!

Narissa didn't put her profile picture and she didn't upload pictures either but it was amazing. She caught up with people from her primary school, people she used to work with and it felt like she had company. She didn't go on the site as much because of time restrictions. Their internet was the old dial up one and she had to connect and then disconnect the internet. She caught up with some news and looked at pictures and what people are up to. It is wonderful. She was asked to put up her profile picture which she finally did and had so many comments like how nice she looked, how pretty and how hot she looked. It made her feel a little more worthy and she was respecting herself again. Are people being real though? Maybe they are all just being kind to her. There is always an element of doubt at the back of her head.

She realised that she had been too absorbed in her own little world of kids, school, and housework and forgotten who she really was and what was worth.

She believed that her children have helped her appreciate herself. Maddie always comments on the beautiful way we dance together and gives her hugs and kisses to tell me how much she loves her mum. Ella loves her food and tells Narissa that her mum is the best cook. Max loves it when they build castles together in the sandpit or with Lego and he loves to help Narissa chop up vegetables and sometimes vacuuming.

Guess who she found on Facebook? Lawrence! He has had Facebook for the last five years and has over 500 friends. That was just unbelievable and yet she was not allowed to be on any social media site due to... not exactly sure why. She was told it was dangerous and people got all your details from your profile.

One rule for Lawrence and another for her!

This is something she had experienced with Lawrence throughout her life. When they used to go to restaurants and set down for a meal, Lawrence would flirt with the waitress and ask personal questions, especially if they were young and pretty. Yet he would be totally rude to the male waiters. He will ask the girl what perfume they wore despite his wife sitting right in front of him and yet he questions pretty waitresses as if he was trying to pick a date. Narissa never understood that.

One day she decided to give his own medicine back. She went for a coffee at this beautiful cafe in the bush setting with a little stream and a park next to it. These were the days before they had children. A handsome young waiter appeared at the table to very politely take their order. Narissa put on a big smile and said "how is your day going?"

"Very well, thank you" he replied with a beaming smile showing his cute deep dimples.

"You guys have been busy today?" Narissa asked still smiling and moving the salt and pepper shakers out of the way and putting them on the edge of the table.

"Yes, it has been rather. I think the nice weather brings everyone out" he replied with his charming smile.

"You have a foreign accent. Let me guess...is it Irish?" Narissa asked with a beaming smile. Lawrence is looking down at the table. His eyes are not lifting off the table top.

"Spot on! OMG you are go-od, you are good. Most people struggle. They think I am Canadian or Scottish or mixed" his smile got bigger and eyes just glittered.

"So you are studying here?" Narissa asked lifting her eyes to meet his. She was beginning to enjoy this. He looked gorgeous with soft tender eyes, with red blonde hair and very nice muscly arms.

A lot of the waiters came from overseas on either exchange programmes or just working visitors permits.

"I am on a working visa for a few months, then I want to travel around and see different parts of Australia and hopefully get to New Zealand" he replied seriously.

"Awesome!" Narissa replied.

"Oh we better give you our order." Narissa could see Lawrence's face twitching and he is clenching his jaw and fists as if he was about to hit someone. His veins were popping out at the side of his head around the temples.

Narissa quickly placed the order as they were only there for coffee. She was getting a cunning plan in her head. 'What if I order lunch and then we will have to stay longer and really piss Lawrence off by shooting off to the ladies, timing it perfectly so that I can bump into this waiter.'

'I couldn't go through with this plan. I am not that cruel.'

'Hell I am beginning to sound like Lawrence' she thought.

As soon as the waiter left, Lawrence pulled her gaze into his and thumped his fists on the table, "what the heck was all that about?" Jeez, he was so demanding!

"I was just making conversation with a foreigner." I took my gaze away from Lawrence to show him that I couldn't care less about his opinion. I had a cheeky smile on my face, one eyebrow raised, looking like a woman in love.

'Okay, this is not going well. Is he feeling what I usually feel? He talks about everything and gets to the point of asking waitresses where they live etc. Sometimes it embarrasses me. I wasn't doing that to him at all.'

They sat in silence for a while. Neither of them looking at each other and just listening to the silence of this bush setting.

Their coffees arrived and Lawrence's hot buttered savoury scones, with Narissa's chocolate mud cake served with a petite flask of yoghurt arrived.

The waiter got flirty now. "Cappuccino for meh ledy, and flat white for you sir."

"A beautiful sliece of Belgium chocolaite mud cake for a true chocolate lover, I can see the ledy has good taste and scones for you sir" the waiter arrived with a cute accent and the melting voice.

Narissa gave a flirty chuckle in return "I love that accent."

She pulled the cake plate towards herself, sliced a small piece of Belgium chocolate mud cake and lifted her chin up, with her eyes closed, she opened her lips wide and placed the slice into her willing mouth, wrapping her lips around the fork and smoothly bringing the fork out of her mouth, tasting the full flavour of thus velvety chocolate. The waiter was standing on her right and watching her. Narissa loves her chocolate and she felt she did all that in real slow motion. He laid his left hand on her shoulder, dropped down towards her ears and whispered "enjoy" in a smooth velvety voice.

She could see that Lawrence was furious. Oh my! She was enjoying it every bit of it. Chocolate always made her feel so whole and herself.

"I am just enjoying my chocolate and this beautiful setting. Aren't you?" Narissa turned around looking at Lawrence.

"Isn't this place gorgeous? I love the water cascading down the trickling stream. It is so fresh out here, isn't it" she added.

Narissa was in her element and was enjoying every bit of this cake. From the corner of her eye she could see the waiter eyeing at them and she knew he wanted to come over and take their empty cups and plates away, not giving anyone else the opportunity to do that.

The young handsome Irish waiter didn't waste any time. He rushed over as soon as he saw Narissa take the last sip of her coffee. She lifted her cup extra high so he knew.

"Is there anything else I can get you guys?" he asked in his velvety voice.

"Did you enjoy the cake, meh ledy?" He almost whispered.

"I most certainly did. It was just the perfect size. Not too big and not too small. I can savour the taste all day now," Narissa flirtatiously replied, putting her head back and absorbing the sun shining over her face, making her skin look more radiant and even younger

"Do you bake the cakes here?" she asked, slightly seriously.

"In fact, some of them are and this particular one is made by our Irish baker and he just invented this recipe recently," he replied with his gentle calm gaze, his eyebrows gently lifting and moving his body closer to Narissa's side again.

Narissa turned and met his eyes. "Well, tell your chef that this is the best cake I have ever had in my life. I really mean that." she gave a slight chuckle.

"You can find us on Facebook and give us a like. Here is our card." He handed the card from the cafe.

"I will. I am certainly going to check it out. Pity I didn't take a picture of the cake." I replied.

"That's ok. You might find pictures on our page. You can like and share." He replied.

With that the waiter left as he got called to another table and Lawrence got up abruptly. "I need to go to the bathroom."

"Ok, I can go and settle the bill," Narissa offered.

She walked to the counter to pay and the waiter came back.

"Any places you recommend for some real cool photography? I have a real passion in photographing landscapes, sunsets, sunrises and animals if I can." He laughed a little.

OMG, this guy is unreal. Narissa has the same passion as him but now she felt a bit scared. 'Should I share my passion with him or not'.

She couldn't help herself. "Me too! I mean I love taking pictures. The trouble with me is that I don't have a good camera. I just use this Sony cyber shot. Don't get me wrong, it takes great photos but ideally I want a long range lens, with unique features like fuzzing the edges and maybe panoramic photos."

"Why don't you get a nice camera then? There are some really good ones out there now." He is getting too interested. Narissa can see Lawrence appearing from the side of the building and seeing us together he rushes up.

"We were just talking about cameras. He was saying how he loves to take photos." I am talking as if trying to get Lawrence interested, fully aware that Lawrence has no hobbies or passions and no interest in photography.

Narissa had planned to buy a nice camera after she they got married, but Lawrence won't let her. Narissa looked at some really great ones and Lawrence kept saying that it was too expensive and that she should wait as people were trying to swindle her. So she gave up looking.

"Anyway, you enjoy your time here and hope you get to explore our beautiful country. We may not see you next time we come here." It was kind of sad.

"Hey, I never say never," he replied with 2 fingers up and both hands gesturing.

As soon as Narissa got into the car seat, Lawrence just took off in great speed. He doesn't say much but when he does it is bad news. 'Ahaa...so you can't take it when I am a little friendly with a waiter but it is ok for you to flirt in front of me with all the waitresses out there' Narisa thought to herself.

Lawrence was a very jealous man which Narissa realised. She was made to feel bad and often enough she did.

The rest of the journey home was in silence.

*"Betrayal was what I felt, my heart broken not just by a guy I was in love with, but also by, as I once believed, a true friend."*

—Danka V.

# CHAPTER 13

*"A self-absorbed person only can see the fault of others,*
*but are often colour-blind to their own"* –Anon

"HONEY, REMEMBER I have to be at Suzie's tonight? She is having a Tupperware sale and I am going to support her."

No answer. When there is no answer Narissa knows that Lawrence is scheming. He doesn't want to be at home doing mundane child minding. To be honest he doesn't want Narissa to go out at all.

For years she held herself back from going out at all. She received a lot of invitations from friends but she wasn't allowed to go. Lawrence always mentioned to her that they were very tight financially and that the kids don't listen to him. 'The kids need their mother' he told her.

Some months ago Narissa was invited to a girl's night out. There were six ladies all from the school and they had planned to go to a movie premiere. The deal was a $9.00 ticket to the movie with a glass of wine with a plate of nibbles to go around as well.

Two of the ladies whom Narissa knew really well asked her twice and they also mentioned that by the time they leave home, the kids would be in bed. They will pick her up from home. The other 3 ladies also from school were known to Narissa.

She was really excited for this night and got herself well organised. She had to work extra hard during the day and because she didn't do this often Narissa always had to double or triple check that she had organised everyone well. For this night out, which was the first time since Ella was born, Narissa was a bit apprehensive at first, only because Ella was 18 months old and she had not left the children alone with Lawrence before. She figured out that the children would be all in bed and there was nothing else to do for Lawrence but just to do what he normally does, sit in front of TV with laptop on his lap and pretend to be working.

Narissa's ride arrived. It was a cold winter's day, she got her old pair of winter boots out, scarf and mittens. She put on the woollen coat. She got into the seven seater Chrysler Voyager and all the ladies went "we are not going skiing!" Narissa obviously overdressed. 'You might get too warm in the theatre, love' came from Brenda, who is the PTA chairperson. They reminded Narissa that the theatre will have heaters on. The car was nice and warm too.

"Well I won't freeze to death then, ha-ha." replied Narissa.

As the car drove off into darkness, Narissa felt really guilty for going out. 'I hope that all the children will sleep soundly while I am out' she thought. Hoping that kids will behave for Lawrence.

They arrived at the cinema complex, a few flight of steps and on the mezzanine floor there were a million people gathered around. The champagne tray arrived followed by a plate of nibbles with chips and dips, carrot and celery sticks and a plate with wedges.

The ladies were all happy chatting away sipping their glasses of champagne and helping themselves to a few. A platter with some pretzels, nuts and chips arrived as well. It felt rather nice to be served for once. Narissa felt like another glass of champagne as she drank hers too fast.

The 7.30 start to the movie was perfect time as children would be all fast asleep but Narissa still felt a bit mushy in her stomach. All the other ladies were enjoying themselves, laughing and noticing everything around them. The upcoming movie posters were up and plans were being made for the other movie night outs. For some reason Narissa wasn't absorbing much. She felt dark, head buzzing with everyone's cheers, laughter and giggles. All the words were just flying around her like bees buzzing around her ears. She was blinking uncontrollably because her body was looking for a resting place. Her legs felt jelly and she felt as though she was far away from everyone.

She knew that this was her first and the last time at the movies. It took her a good hour to get into the movie. She was physically sitting with everyone but felt no one. She felt totally out and alone. The story line and the movie itself felt foreign to her. She felt as though she might have dozed off with her eyes open.

All she could hear was Maddie's voice and Lawrence arguing with her, Lawrence hitting her, Maddie crying, Max shutting his door on everyone and Ella sleeping.

At half time the ladies were all chatting about the slow moving movie. Narissa escaped to the bathroom which had a long queue. She managed to get in and by the time she got back, her group had left for the seats.

"We were looking for you?" said Helen.

"We thought you might have had problems at home." Maria added.

"All good. I had to get to the ladies and there was a queue" Narissa whispered.

"You enjoying yourself, love?" asked Brenda. "You seem a bit tired."

"I am ok, thanks guys. I have not left the children with Lawrence before" Narissa replied.

"He is home then?" asked Maria. "Because he does work very late, doesn't he?" she added.

For once Lawrence was on time. When Narissa had reluctantly agreed to go out that night, she had asked Lawrence and then told him that Helen was coming to pick her up with the other ladies so he couldn't be late. Surprisingly enough, for once he was not late.

On the way back home when the ladies were sharing their view point about the movie, Narissa felt like a sleepy teenager in an English class, not having done her homework.

She just said it was an interesting movie. Seemed like she hadn't understood what the movie was about.

Narissa was glad to be dropped off at home and stepped out quickly. With a big smile she thanked everyone and waved goodbye to all the girls and slowly made her way up the drive to the front door. She turned the key to the door and at the same time listening to any sign of life in the house. All was quiet and she felt great. Phew! Lawrence must have had a quiet night.

She walked into the lounge quietly and there he was in front of his computer with TV on.

"Oh Hi, you still up? Did the children behave themselves?" Narissa asked in a quite comforting voice.

"How much did this evening cost you?" he replied in a condescending voice. The tone of his voice made her think that he was angry.

Narissa stood still with disbelief. 'Did I hear what I think I heard?'

She was about to sit down but now felt like a small school child ready to be reprimanded for foolishness. 'Actually I think he is a bigger fool' she thought to herself. She just stared at Lawrence who wouldn't even lift his head to look at her.

Narissa always felt obliged to remain positive and never take unnecessary comments from other people and belittle herself.

She was wrong to be thinking that Lawrence would be interested to know how she went, did she enjoy her first outing with ladies of her age group and having a laugh. But she was wrong! He wanted to know how much this evening cost her. Where is this even coming from?

Narissa sat down and said "how was your evening?" in a very soft caring voice.

He hasn't even looked at her since she arrived back from her outing. His head is buried deep in his computer screen and he is typing away. Then he gives a chuckle and smiles and gives a small laugh, throwing his head back.

It took Narissa a few seconds to realise that he was chatting to someone on the computer. What a prick! So he is not going to pay her attention. In other words there is no "us". He doesn't care about her.

These are the times Narissa realises that she is alone in this relationship and have never felt the love or the emotional support from Lawrence.

She got up slowly and as she rose from the sofa, she whispered "$9.00. $9.00 is what the price of my evening was."

Anyway, not feeling wanted she left the room.

While brushing her teeth she felt like an idiot to be thinking that Lawrence cared. Her hands were shaking as she was brushing her teeth. 'Why am I bothering with a wanker like this? If $9.00 going to break his bank balance, so be it!' She thought with anger building inside her.

'Considering I was earning my own money before I married him, and had money saved up in what became a joint account. The passwords for this joint account has changed so now I have no way of knowing how much money we have in the account.' Narissa felt totally useless. Her evening was not enjoyable.

'Oh I see. He has provided me with a house that we built together with my money too! I have a car and food on my table and that means I have to stop living life.' She felt emotions rising up her chest and tears forming in her eyes.

She got herself into bed quietly and just let her mind wonder to her next day's events, planning and working out all the logistics.

Narissa found out one day that Lawrence goes to after work social club and enjoys drinks, plays pool and sometimes goes out for dinner with his work mates and their spouses. This information just landed on her lap as they were out at a garden centre. Narissa wanted to get a cherry blossom plant for the front yard and asked Lawrence if they could go together. He had agreed because Lawrence sometimes likes to please Narissa.

One of Lawrence's workmate was at the garden centre wheeling his son in a wheelbarrow. Lawrence would never do that with a wheelbarrow that belonged to the shop. This 4 year old kid seemed to be enjoying himself with big smiles, arms waving around, having a lot of fun. Narissa smiled at this child as they drove past them. This kid had let his arms out to snap Narissa and she let him. "Weeee ha-ha weee yippee! Dad, we haven't crashed yet!"

Lawrence recognised the father "Hey mate" he called out.

The guy stopped the wheelbarrow and gently lowered it to the ground. "I came here to pick up bathroom fittings and I have not made it to the aisle yet. Can you believe it, we have been here for almost an hour, hehe" he chuckled.

He then extended his arm to introduce himself. "I am Mark and you must be Lawrence's other half. I believe we have never met"

Lawrence never feels the need to introduce Narissa to his work mates. Usually Narissa introduces herself but she had no idea where Mark was from. Narissa just stayed to one side.

"Very well, mate" Mark replied.

Then turning towards Narissa "We didn't see you ag-ain! Last night was great!" Mark said with great excitement.

Then turning towards Lawrence, "Wasn't it, mate?" Mark is beaming with smiles and patted Lawrence on the shoulder.

Lowering his head, Lawrence looked at Narissa for a second and then with great enthusiasm and a change of voice he went on "oh yeah, last night."

"We were at this new restaurant after social club and my wife Julie made it. You should come sometime." Mark responded casually.

"We do this every 5th Friday. Our social club organises games and drinks and then we go out for a bite. By that stage all our spouses can join us." Mark tells me.

"Oh no. I don't work and I am not in the city. I have 3 young children at home." I said stumbling my words and feeling a bit awkward.

"Hey, my wife Julie doesn't work either but we get a babysitter for a couple of hours. It gets her out of the house as Julie, like yourself is full time at home with the children. She needs an outlet, you know." Mark replied.

"Look at her, she was out last night and this morning she is getting a Pedicure, while I am supposedly looking for bathroom fittings" haha. He gives a short laugh and makes everything seem so chilled and relaxed.

I just nodded my head "yeah, sure. When Lawrence lets me know" Narissa threw a glance at Lawrence. She never knew that this was happening. 'Why would Lawrence keep this from her?' she thought.

"What are you doing, man? Bring her out!" Mark called patting Lawrence on the shoulder again.

Turning towards Narissa "you will enjoy it because all the ladies are in the same boat as us...you know young family. Julie would love to share experiences with you. She is always telling me she needs someone to do things with."

'Gosh, Mark has no idea who he is talking to. I felt like screaming out "damn you! I am a KEPT woman' because now that's what Narissa was feeling like.

She just smiled and said "sure! Would love to meet Julie."

"I guess we shouldn't hold you any longer. Looks like someone wants to carry on this fun activity" Narissa replied. She brushed her hands over this kid's hair and he jumped up and down in his wheelbarrow "c'mon dad, let's go!"

Off they went.

'Did I just get more insight into the man I married? I know that life is a journey and you find things about each other as life evolves but I don't understand why Lawrence would never mention this to me.' Narissa thought.

'He has been going out for dinners with other couples on his own while I have been at home cooking him meals on a Friday night and waiting for him to turn up?

No wonder, sometimes he turns up and 8 or close to 9 and says "what a busy day!" Then he will sit with me at the dining table pretending to not have eaten at all. Why?' Narissa feels really cheated.

'Is there a problem with me? Do I look ugly and not worthy of Lawrence's love? Why can't Lawrence be honest with me?' Narissa started to question herself.

'My friend Fifi has three children and her husband works away a lot. In fact he owns a share in his company and Fifi works really hard with the children. She is at home with the children like me. She takes Gemma to Ballet and the boys to swimming lessons, gymnastics, karate and music lessons. Fifi doesn't have to go out to work but when Greg is home he takes kids to school and sometimes sends Fifi off to Melbourne for a weekend of shopping. Greg does all the running around himself. How does he know what to do?' Narissa is trying very hard to figure out what is wrong in their relationship. She blamed herself because Lawrence blames her for everything.

Narissa asked Fifi once how she makes Greg help around. "I write it all down and Greg just follows." She says it so casually.

"Damn, Fifi, if I write it like this for Lawrence he tells me that I treat him like a child. Yet, at the same time he doesn't listen and won't bother helping out. I don't know how to say to him that I need a break too" Narissa had told her.

Last time Narissa was at Fifi's for a coffee, she showed her all the beautiful clothes, shoes, perfume and make up she bought in Melbourne. "Well, Greg booked me into a hotel right next to the DFO (Direct factory outlet) and it was a plush place with cooked breakfast every day. Look, I brought these slippers and gown back, hehe." Fifi was acting like a teenage girl with her purchases, but it was great to see someone so happy.

Narissa loved Fifi, she was a real good friend, a true friend. She is not the show off type and they always had so much to talk about.

The only thing Narissa can't talk to her friends about is the relationship or lack of it that she has with Lawrence.

The only outing Narissa ever had with Lawrence was when they went for family dinners and that means organising herself and looking after the children when they are with the family. The other times are when she goes out shopping for furniture or garden products.

Ella is growing fast and getting too big for her cot. It is an old fashioned but a very solid built cot which had seen three children through but Ella really needed her own bed.

While playing the pole tennis with the kids in the front yard Narissa managed to talk to Louise, the neighbour's daughter from across the road to help baby sit the children while her and Lawrence went out looking for a bed.

Louise is in year 10 at school and wants to drop out to be a baker. She has 2 younger siblings and there is like an 8 year gap between her and her younger sister. Louise doesn't get on that well with her mum at this point in life and last time Narissa had spoken with Helena, she suggested that Louise could baby sit for her for an hour or 2 at a time for some pocket money. Louise was looking for work but with no experience on hand she was finding it difficult.

Narissa was happy to help out because like Helena suggested $5 an hour was good enough.

Narissa suggested to Lawrence that instead of dragging the kids to furniture store, she will get Louise to baby sit one Saturday afternoon while they went out to look for a bed for Ella. This took a lot of courage for Narissa to do because Lawrence is always angry with Narissa.

Lawrence is never happy when it comes to spending money on children or anything to do with the family. The very first shop they entered and Narissa had barely taken 2 steps into the shop, when a tall skinny late 40's woman came running towards them full of excitement, ravishingly licking her lips, boobs bouncing and arms stretched out as if greeting a lover. "Ohh Law-rie! Sooo good to see you! Where have you be-een? It has been a while, hasn't it" rolling her eyes.

She is now hugging her husband and kissing him and rubbing herself against him.

Narissa froze. She was shocked. She stood there, blinking her eyes, thinking to herself that she has never met this woman, don't know her, never seen her.

Lawrence doesn't know where to look. When his eyes start darting like a bird Narissa is almost sure that he is lying and he is feeling like he has been caught out.

Narissa threw a disgusting glance at them both but started to walk away.

"This man makes the best cocktails. The best in town. Trust me. I know" this haggard says as if she has been out with Lawrence on dates.

Lawrence ignores Narissa as he doesn't know what to say. She walked away and not sure what to say or do herself. The best solution was to walk away.

'Sure, this lady is mistaken, but she had called him Lawrie. I am sure Lawrence will explain to me later' thought Narissa.

If she had asked anything about this lady in front of Lawrence he would have out her down in front of this lady and made Narissa feel like a possessive wife as he had done to her before. The best way Lawrence likes it is not to ask him anything, which Narissa did.

She quickly looked around the shop and didn't like anything. Perhaps she had a disgusting feeling and that turned her off looking at the furniture in a more favourable way. She turned around and saw Lawrence standing in the same spot, frozen and looking sheepishly around. This skinny wrinkled face slut with sloppy boobs was still chatting with him. Then she heard them both laugh and chatting away.

At that stage Narissa got a bit annoyed.

At least I have firmer boobs, thanks to my 3 children.

Narissa spoke from about 5 meters away as there wasn't anyone else in the shop "Shall we go. I haven't seen anything I like here" she said it with no emotion. With Lawrence's treatment over the years she has become quite unemotional and especially after what she had just encountered she was feeling sick in her stomach.

What she really felt like doing was grabbing the car keys off Lawrence and driving home without him. Leave him with this unattractive skinny bitch. 'I am so weak, don't have the guts to hurt anyone' Narissa thought. Instead she went outside and waited by the car.

Lawrence came out of the shop almost 10 minutes after her. He unlocked the car. "What was the other shop you wanted to go?" he asks with a sheepish voice.

'Right now I want to put a bullet through his heart. I am thinking of my children, of Fifi whose husband treats her like a princess, of all my friends who have loving husbands who would never even look at another woman.' Thought Narissa who was feeling a little hurt now.

Couldn't he just fill her in on what happened in there?

'Lawrence has been making cocktails for other women? When? When he has been working late, is that when? When he is working away in another city?

But...this woman works in a furniture shop. She is a salesperson! Where would Lawrence have met her? Has to be at a bar?' Narissa is beginning to feel really cheated on now.

Her eyes were totally filled with tears but she better not blink. If she blinks the tears will roll down her cheeks and according to Lawrence women who cry are weak. Her eyes are blurry and she can't focus. She turned her head towards the window so she is not looking at Lawrence. She can't stand him right now. How dare he break that trust!

Before they got married, Lawrence had said to Narissa that he wanted to start this relationship with honesty and always be faithful with each other.

Narissa can't help herself and her nose is now filling like a soda machine. She blinked and sighed with little huffs of cry spewing out. At the back of her head she was reminding herself that she was not weak, just so that she could hold these damn tears back.

"I would rather go home. I don't want to meet any more of your cocktail escorts or women you have bedded! How dare you! You are a fucking piece of shit! You are a lying, pathetic, cheating swine! I hate you today and I will hate you for the rest of my life!" Narissa blurted out with anger and vengeance.

She was feeling real low and it was so hard to explain how her heart was throbbing right now.

"I don't know her." Lawrence replied. "I don't even know her name" he added.

"Excuse me! You don't know her? She comes running to you, kissing you and telling me you make the best cocktails in town? You stood there not saying anything!

"I didn't hear you say 'I don't know you'" Narissa exhaled her words out in panted anger.

"You think I am stupid? Do you Lawrence? Honestly! Can you look me in the eye and tell me all this happened before we got married?" Narissa asked him questioningly.

"Honestly, I don't know her. I don't remember where I have met her." That was Lawrence's pathetic reply.

"She works in a furniture shop. She doesn't work with you! You have some explaining to do" Narissa replied and sat stern in the car.

"I want to go home now" she reprimanded.

Lawrence didn't offer any more explanations nor did he tell Narissa what he talked about and basically left it at that.

They drove home silently. Narissa can feel the knife edge between them.

The best method of coping for Lawrence is to ignore everything. He doesn't feel the need to explain anything to Narissa. He thinks it is his right to stay quiet and that Narissa, his wife doesn't need any explanations from him for his actions.

The garage door opened and Narissa without wasting time jumped out of the car. The kids come running out to meet their mum. Ella was jumping up and down thinking they had a bed in the boot of the car. Maddie is running around the car. "Where is it? Where is Ella's bed?"

Ella is just jumping up and down clapping her hands, "new bed, and new bed."

"We didn't get one today, darlings. We couldn't find the right size." Narissa knelt down to hug the kids. They were her world. They were honest and ever so giving of love. No matter how much pain and hurt she suffered. Just holding the children in her arms always made it all melt away.

"You guys are so stupid! How do you think we can fit a bed in this car?" Lawrence screams out. He is so insensitive. He doesn't understand kids at all.

'Perhaps he should just go and make more cocktails for this skinny boobless, wrinkly bitch' thought Narissa.

Just then Louise came over. "How did you go?"

"By the way Lawrence, kids don't have concept of space or how things fit into things till they try it themselves. Trust me, I know. Having two younger siblings I have learnt that" Louise told Lawrence.

Lawrence can get some real life lessons from this 16 year old.

Narissa paid Louise who could tell that there was tension between Narissa and Lawrence. "Oh my god! You have been crying. Are you ok? Mum is home. You want to come and have a chat with mum? She will make you a cuppa."

Louise couldn't hold herself. She is so grown up.

Narissa really didn't want to go right now and sit to talk about her findings. It seems like every time she is out with Lawrence she uncovers more about his liaisons with other people and it isn't always good.

She is really beginning to think that she has something lacking that Lawrence has to hide little things from her. She can't understand why Lawrence wouldn't share his interactions with his own wife.

'I am so angry right now. I still can't believe that he had been out partying with some old bitch. How can he!' Narissa is beating herself up for never questioning Lawrence about his late nights. He had told her that he was working and if she didn't believe him then there was no relationship. Narissa always trusted him, perhaps too much.

She started tidying up kids toys which she doesn't normally do. She is banging and throwing toys in the toy boxes angrily. She feels like packing his things and throwing him out tonight.

'At least he can give me an explanation, put my mind at ease' she thought.

Ella walked up and sat on Narissa's lap. She took a whiff of her sweet perfumed hair and caressed her hair while thinking what to do. Leaving Lawrence crossed her mind.

'If I leave today, how am I going to pack up all the children's things and where will I go.' she thought sadly.

Ella knows when Narissa is unhappy. She will hug her real strong. Maddie runs up and almost bulldozes them both over. She is very strong. "Mumma, when will you get Ella a bed?" Maddie asked in a very caring voice.

"Mumma, we got all the sheets ready and everything ready with Louise" Maddie says in a motherly voice.

Kids are so innocent. Narissa kissed both her girls on the forehead one by one, first Ella then Maddie. After a while they went to the spare room and started playing with the glitter and making rainbow with the coloured pens. Narissa had a room all set up with paints, paper, scissors and everything you need for collage or craft work. This was their chilling out room, very therapeutic.

After a while Ella is hungry.

Ella lets Narissa know whenever she is hungry. Maddie will eat when she is called and Max is not fussed. Narissa quickly got the tiny pots of yoghurt out and while they were all sitting at the little table eating, she cut up some apples and cheese and got the crackers out. She made 2 cups of tea.

'Why two? Even though I hate Lawrence so much today, I am still a human being and as usual I have made him a cup of tea and a muffin to go with it' Narissa thought. Can't put this incident out of her head today.

She asked Maddie to call dad, even though she has no idea where he is. Maddie said she had seen him outside talking to the neighbour about cutting down some trees.

Cutting down trees? Narissa had asked Lawrence ages ago about pruning the big sweet pea tree down which was blocking the sunlight and being dangerous in high winds. He had said that it didn't need chopping. There was a flyer in the letter box from a tree loping company and Narissa was going to ask them for a quote but Lawrence had shut her down.

He had told her that the tree was no danger and that there was no issue with the sunshine. Now he was looking at getting the tree cut down? 'Unbelievable' she thought.

Lawrence doesn't come in so Narissa just walked outside the back patio and left his tea and muffin on the table under the covered area of the patio. She should see Lawrence, pointing to the top branches of the tree trying to impress Amanda, the next door neighbour, making it look like it was all his idea. Wow!

Anyway, he has seen Narissa so he came over "Darling, I was just saying to Amanda that we will cut the top branches of this sweet pea tree, maybe next weekend. We haven't got any plans, have we?" he asks in a very sweet polite voice as if they were the best of couples and he has so much respect for his wife.

"Amanda reckons it is a great idea and it will give them more sunlight too just like we had discussed the other day" he added.

Wow, unbelievable! He has suggested to cut the tree down for more sunlight? 'Darling? Seriously Lawrence?' Narissa is amazed.

Amanda has no idea what she has been through this afternoon. What Narissa has discovered about her husband's lying cheating character.

'Yes, sure. The sooner the better." Narissa brushed it off.

"See you Amanda. I am just feeding the kids."

"No problems. We will have coffee one day." Amanda replied. She know how busy Narissa is with her 3 under 5 years of age children. Amanda has 3 of her own but her husband is very involved with the family.

After cleaning the dishes, tidying up the kitchen, Narissa got the washing in, folded them and then got the kids to put them in their draws. She started with dinner. It seems that each time she is alone she can see this skinny old bitch enjoying herself with her husband having cocktails while Narissa was at home alone waiting for him. She obviously has full on busy days with the children and have no help, naturally tired by the end of the day which is around 11 sometimes, even then she makes an effort to stay up and wait for Lawrence to come home.

'He has been having cocktails! He has never made cocktails for me, NEVER!' she thought.

To lie about having to work late, is something Narissa can't tolerate. 'What else is he hiding from me,' she thought.

She almost chopped off her fingers while shredding the cabbage, because she is very distracted. Her mind is full of disturbing thoughts. Narissa always reminds herself that there the only way to keep her sanity is to ask for forgiveness. She thought maybe she had something wrong.

Today the family was having grilled chicken, jacket potatoes and cabbage salad Narissa learnt to make from a Cambodian friend. Today she had no pleasure in cooking for Lawrence but her kids came first. Regardless, she can't let her inner turmoil have any effect on the children. Something she will never do.

Narissa planned to talk to Lawrence after the kids had all gone to bed. She thought that was the best she could do for now. She had to pretend that everything was fine.

Another day over and after her shower, she was ready for bed. Lawrence is already in bed, reading something pretending to be of great importance. Narissa got into bed and he doesn't even look at her. He continued to read and pretend as though he had not seen Narissa get into bed.

'Where did all the showy darling affection go?' she thought.

"So is this tree being chopped off because Amanda wants it cut?" Gosh I have so much hate in me Narissa thought.

"Well, she brought it up." Lawrence has lost his politeness again.

"I thought you said it was unnecessary" replied Narissa.

"Well, it has grown a lot, since" he replied.

In one week the tree had taken off like that. Narissa is bewildered.

"You want to explain about this woman in the shop today?" Her voice is becoming hurtful but this time for herself.

"What do you want to know? I told you, I don't know her!"

"Stop shouting at me. I have the right to know who you are out with and when. I am your wife." She replied hastily.

'Maybe he thinks I am a kept woman' Narissa wonders.

"There is nothing to tell." He switches his lights off, rolls over to one side and falls asleep.

Lawrence will avoid and leave Narissa hanging like this. The pain and suffering inside her indicated that he doesn't care. He doesn't care what impact it has on her and how it affects her mental emotional health.

So that's it.

Narissa spent hours lying in bed with no closure on her emotional discomfort today. Wondered if all the times and days he told her that he was working late, he was actually out enjoying himself? No wonder he is so cagey about their bank accounts. Narissa wasn't allowed to see their accounts.

'I despise him' she thought.

Unfortunately, this feeling was hindering her from falling asleep. She tossed and turned several times, the bed felt uncomfortable and she was irritated listening to Lawrence snore his night away.

There was nothing she could do except try to get some sleep. She tried to talk to God, she had conversations with herself, like in the book "Conversations with God."

It took her a long time to fall asleep but she must have fallen asleep in the early hours of the morning.

"One lie is enough to question all truths"

# CHAPTER 14

*"When you do something with a lot of honesty, appetite and commitment, the input reflects in the output."* A. R. Rahman

'MY GOODNESS WHAT a winter! It had been really wet and very cold. We had one lot of sickness this winter and that's not bad. We only had slight sniffles and temperatures but nothing major. I swear by Homeopathy. It is the best form of medication for the family. It is cheap, effective and there are no side effects. Kids absolutely love it which makes it so much easier to administer' Narissa is sitting by the window absorbing the warmth from the sun.

She thought that it was time to sit and chat with her husband. Therefore, she called him at work one day and he was ever so polite. She couldn't believe her ears, "hello darling, how is it going? Everything alright?" with an accent that was so cheekily amazing.

Narissa was speechless. The voice was familiar but not the tone. The chocolaty voice and the mannerism was too different to what she was used to at home. She blinked her eyes in disbelief and hesitantly said "oh um we are um all good, um thanks. Just wanted to say that..." she started to stammer and the words were disappearing from her head. Her lips were quivering to deliver the words and the brain was shutting down. The words were floating in her head like butterflies and she was giving it her best to catch them.

"Well" *after a long pause*, "I was thinking that we haven't been out in a while and... mum was saying that there is a great movie on. *Pause*...Did you want to go? *Pause* I know we are low on funds and all but we can get cheap seats and mum can look after the children as she is always offering. It just means that we don't have to pay for babysitting" Gosh, she said that all in a quick sentence.

"We can have early dinner and then head off to the movies, we don't have to go out for dinner" Narissa quickly added her heart beating fast and she was feeling like a small child who was trying to justify her actions.

Right now she wasn't feeling good. That's not what she had planned to say at all. Her imagination took the better of me. She had actually prepared a very different question and rehearsed it several times in her head all morning. What she really meant to say was "you have been working a lot recently. Do you think you can come home a bit early and have a discussion about 'stuff'? I get really tired by the time you get home and we don't seem to talk much. It means I don't have any idea about spending and all."

"Oh yeah, sounds like a great idea! Just tell me when and we can do that. Just brilliant!"

Did I hear that correctly? "Ok, I will check to see what times and which cinema."

"See you at home. Love ya." The phone goes dead. "Do I believe that this can actually happen, going to the movies with my husband?" Narissa can't believe that. He is usually very rude and cruel to her but in public he is a different person.

It is pretty obvious that he is among people at work and shows them that he is a nice man.

'I am too nice and always believe in the power of positive thinking' thought Narissa.

She looked at the movies and the one that mum was talking about is not in cinemas any more. She had to find another one to watch. Actually Narissa's mum had mentioned about this movie a while back, maybe 2 or more months ago so naturally it would be over by now.

There happened to be a good one on Friday night at 7.30pm. This meant mum could come over and have dinner with them.

Well, Narissa hadn't seen Lawrence much since she had spoken to him about the movies at work and he hadn't mentioned the movies either. She was not sure whether to inform mum that she might have to babysit that Friday or to wait till it was really happening because with Lawrence, he may agree to something but it never eventuate.

Wednesday morning she quickly ran behind him as he was just about to get into the car. "Do you still want to go to the movies? The one that mum talked about has finished. She told me some months ago, but there is another one we can go to. I need to ask mum to baby-sit so I have to tell her as soon as possible in case she has other commitments" Narissa asks quickly.

"Well, I have a busy week. You know my job is so demanding, I cannot tell you right now" replied Lawrence and starts the car engine.

Oh, he is so abrupt and the tone of the voice is different and mannerism is like I am annoying him. Not the same person that I spoke to on the phone a few days ago. So he works all the time, even on a Friday night?

What a letdown!

'I can't go anywhere with my family, friends or by myself. After speaking to me so nicely, he turns around and talks like this. What have I done?' Narissa can't stop wondering.

She realised that he has two faces. At work he is the most charming man. No wonder all the women at his work gather around him like he is the most adorable man.

At a work function one day, which Narissa got invited to out of the blue which by the way never happened, this lady who worked at the reception came up and said to Narissa "He is a really nice man, so gentle and caring. He is just so amazingly knowledgeable and helpful."

Narissa doesn't know this man she is talking about. The man she knew before their marriage was a bit like that but not the man she is with now.

He talks gently, calmingly and with a lot of passion, only at work. At home he is in a different mood. It seems like he doesn't want to interact with family members at all. He pushes everyone away all the time.

There's nothing Narissa can say or do when Lawrence has to shoot her off like this. If she demands him to make a decision, he gets twitchy. He calls her a nagging wife.

Narissa closed the door to the internal access garage and slowly made her way up to the kitchen. The feeling is depressing and yet she has to put up a smiley face for the children. Maddie comes up and says "what's wrong, mum? You look sad."

Narissa didn't think it was that obvious. She just smiled and said, "I was thinking what we can do today. I was sad because dad can't join us. He has to work." Narissa is beginning to lie herself now.

'What is in this marriage? Nothing, apart from kids. I don't have time to think about myself.' Narissa thought despairingly.

She feels like she is on such a yo-yo. Every day she has to make all the decisions herself, look after the 3 children and the house plus her studies. Narissa has to take care of the inside and the outside of the house. She has the task of attending to everyone's emotional needs, run the kids to their appointments and their activities and then to deal with a husband who doesn't show any care or respect.

"A smile is the best way to deal with difficult situations. Even if it's a fake one. Used properly, you can fool anyone with them." — Sai

# CHAPTER 15

*"Actions prove who someone is but words just
prove who they pretend to be"* —Anon

ALENTINE'S DAY IS fast approaching and there are some great movies on. Narissa would love to watch "Monsoon Wedding", on a big screen cinema and enjoy a child free romantic night out with Lawrence. She is trying too hard to make this marriage work.

"Honey, what say we go out to movies on Valentine's Day? This year Valentine's Day falls on a Friday and I feel it is just perfect. I talked to my friend, Jane whose niece Kim is looking for extra pocket money and she won't hesitate to mind the children for a few hours." Narissa explained to Lawrence.

Kim had done this for them before and thankfully the kids love her as much as she loves them. The only problem is Maddie can get a bit over the top with her expression of love. Maddie will continue playing 'hide and seek', reading books, playing scrabble or 'I spy" games with Kim. Kim will lose track of time, but Narissa doesn't really care because it is a Friday night and if Maddie has a late night, it wouldn't matter too much.

As normal, she rushed around all day, got all her chores done. After picking the children from school, she popped over to the library. They returned all their books and there must have been at least twenty, mostly Maddie's collection. Max loved his comic books. At such a young age of two, Max was fascinated by the comic books. He loved looking at the pictures and making up his own stories. Ella didn't mind what she got and usually Narissa helped her pick out books, which were usually two to three in total. Maddie on the other and will pick at least twenty. As many as her arms could scoop. Arms wrapped around the books, all close to her chest, barely able to see where she is going, tongue poked out to a side, Maddie will make her way to the counter. She had to be the first in the queue.

Narissa arrived at the counter, got the library card out and the librarian tells her that they have a fine for $7.50. "Are you sure? "We brought all the books back" Narissa replied questioningly.

"You did and it had an overdue book" replied the librarian.

'Oh my! This is why I discourage Maddie from getting twenty books. But she won't listen so I end up paying $7.50, not feeling good about myself.'

Few meters down the road is a little cafe which Narissa and the kids loved. The family have never been to the cafe with Lawrence.

Narissa was so lucky to find a park right outside the cafe. The kids were very excited. Ella is moving up and down in her car seat. She loves the little cookies and Max loves his milk frothy. Narissa hasn't got Max out of his car seat and Maddie is already in the cafe. Narissa just caught a glimpse of Maddie from her back as she entered the cafe. In her pink chequered dress and bouncing along the wooden floor of the porch Maddie is in. The Geraniums are in full bloom, reds, pinks and whites. The cafe has a homely appearance and the staff are ever so friendly. The smell of coffee is divine and the aroma from the homemade soups, breads, scones and cakes are delicious. The olfactory nerves won't miss this at all.

Narissa always sat at the back of this L shaped cafe which is always busy. As she enters the cafe, she realised that Maddie has already given her order as there is a number on the table.

As Narissa brought Ella and Max in, Maddie yells out "here mum! I have a table for us."

Maddie is very clever indeed. She knows exactly what to do.

The friendly staff smile at us as they have got to know us really well. Narissa placed her order and made her way to the side of the cafe, past the shelves loaded with freshly baked breads, scones and cakes. She took a quick glance at the cake shelves as she walked past. The staff know that she only has water and the kids have frothy milk which is 50c and sometimes they will have a small snack of scone or a sandwich to share. Narissa cannot purchase food outside because Lawrence screams at her for wasting money.

She sat down at the table with a sigh and noticed this man at the table opposite them. She recognises him from their previous visits. He has a dark heavy moustache and deep dimples. When he smiles his dimples deepen and he looks gorgeous. She smiled back, just being polite. Then she looked down at her phone, quickly sending a message to Lawrence to remind him of their date that night. The movie starts at 7.30pm and Kim will arrive by 5.45-6pm. By that stage Narissa will have fed the children, bathed them and ready for bed before Kim arrives. She had already prepared diner for tonight which means she can relax a bit when she gets home.

The back door of the cafe leads to a small playground with a swing set and a sliding set. Not far from the back fence of the cafe is a small stream. Kids love this area because they can throw stones and sticks into the stream.

Narissa always does something special with the children on a Friday to finish the week off in a nice way. She loved taking them out to their little favourite places like the library or the park.

Her water arrived, Maddie's food arrived and she didn't realise she had ordered a chicken, avocado toasted sandwich for herself. Ella is happy with her little chocolate cookie which is complimentary with her frothy milk. Narissa ordered a cheese scone which Max loves. Ella has bits of food from Maddie and Max and that is enough for her while Narissa sticks with water.

The kids ate fast and they left to play outside. Narissa can see them from where she is and she took her time to pack up tissues, put everything in an organised manner. She liked to pile up the plates, the utensils and cups so the staff at the cafe have an easier time clearing the table.

As she was about to get up to go outside this man in the heavy moustache approaches Narissa. "Hi" he said in a deep voice.

"Oh hey." Narissa replied abruptly not knowing what he wanted from her. 'If he is going to start giving me advice, I am outta here.' she thought. She cannot tolerate people who think they know everything and start handing out unnecessary advice.

He drew his right arm out and she extended hers to have a handshake except he won't let go of Narissa's hand. His eyes are glued on her and she was feeling rather uneasy. She tried to pull her hand away but his grip was very strong. Narissa didn't want to pull too hard looking like an over reactive highly emotional mother, so she smiled and pulled her hand gently. He was still smiling and said "Your kids are beautiful...just like their mother, huh."

Narissa stopped smiling. He was actually a good looking man in his late thirties, maybe forty and has a nice brown leather jacket. But he made her feel so vulnerable. He reminded her of Magnum P.I. And she loved Magnum P.I at one stage. Narissa thought Tom Selleck was a hunky man, her heart throb in her teenage years.

"Sorry, I have to go and chase the children." She gave a quick side glance and with a lump in her throat, she repeated, "sorry, I have to go and chase the children."

He didn't say anything but pulled his hand back slowly and the gentle graze of his hands made her quiver.

She hurriedly packed everything in her bag, pushed the chair in against the table and left the cafe through the back door. She stepped outside and as usual, Maddie had Ella on the swing and her and Max were taking turns to push her. Ella is laughing and tilts her head back to glance at me. Narissa suddenly realised that she hadn't paid her bill.

She quickly told the children that she has to go back to pay the bill and will be back soon and told the children to be careful and then stepped back into the cafe to pay her bill. Sarah, the girl at the counter said "that man who was talking to you has already paid your bill."

'Okay it wasn't much but I didn't feel good. I looked around and couldn't see him anywhere.'

"Sarah, where did he go?"

Narissa asked worriedly.

"Oh, He left" she replied.

Gosh! Narissa couldn't even thank him and she was not sure if she wants to see him again. Something inside her wanted to meet him again just so she could thank him.

"He didn't have to do that" Narissa exclaimed. Sarah just smiled.

Narissa stepped outside, the grass was a bit overgrown. This place at the back of the cafe was very nice, with the sun setting down and the green grass looked yellow from the rays of the sun. The water in the stream sparkled as it flowed down. The kids were enjoying themselves. So she let them all have a turn on the swing while she pushed the swing back and forth. She couldn't get this man's face out of her head. His smile, his gaze and the handshake just made her heart miss beats. She smiled and hoped nobody was looking at her. Narissa also didn't like receiving this type of kindness from people.

Unfortunately all good things must come to an end and it was time to go back home, back to all the chores. Kim arrived at 5.30pm and that was just such a blessing. Narissa was a lot slower today, maybe because this man's face in her head was holding her back. She was wondering why he would pay her bill. She didn't like this gesture.

Kim is happy to stay the night. She said "you don't have to pay me any extra. When Lawrence comes home, just go out for a meal before movies and I am happy to stay the night."

Kim knows we have a spare bedroom downstairs or pull a mattress in Maddie's room. It felt like everything was going really well. The kids would have burnt enough energy to sleep well tonight.

Narissa was ready to feed the children, and get them organised but Kim won't let Narissa do that. She tells Narissa to go and get ready.

"I have a lot of time, Kim" Narissa told her.

Kim and Narissa were chatting and Narissa was happy, whether from the thought of a stranger telling her that she had beautiful children or the thought of going out tonight. Usually when she is going out with Lawrence she is a bit anxious, stressed and sometimes guilty. Lawrence makes very cutting remarks sometimes and she is never sure what mood he will be in tonight. Narissa was a lot relaxed because she had Kim with her, an extra pair of hands and someone who was able to give an opinion like an adult.

Maddie came out of bed, dragging her little comfort T-shirt. She has taken to one of Narissa's favourite green T-shirt with black writing all over. Maddie keeps this T-shirt by her side and carries it with her to the lounge or to bed. Narissa had washed it a few times so it isn't smelly or anything. She rubs her eyes and comes over, "mu-mmy, when are you going?" In her most sweetest little voice. "You look pretty."

Narissa looked up at the clock and it was already 6.45pm. She was beginning to panic now. She called Lawrence and there was no reply. She left a message to say "I am ready and I hope you are on your way. Please call if there is any problems."

Narissa stretched out her arms to lure Maddie into her arms. "Common then" She embraced Maddie and held her in her arms, her head against her bosom and gently kissing her on her forehead.

Little girls are not meant to worry about mums like this.

Lying with Maddie in her bed, curling her hair with soft strokes, Narissa started telling her a story. Her favourite was a made up story adopted from Mary had a little lamb. Narissa made up stories as she went. Her stories would end and if Maddie was still awake, she would start adding more to it. This particular night Mary went to school with her baby lamb for show and tell. Narissa was up to the point where it was school break up time and she could hear Maddie's breathing getting heavier. She knew instantly that Maddie was fast asleep.

In the dark of her room, Narissa tip toed out making sure not to bang or trip on anything as that would wake Maddie up. She was a light sleeper.

Sitting in the lounge, looking at the clock with so much disappointment, Narissa felt really awkward when Kim entered the lounge "Aren't you guys going out tonight?"

"Lawrence isn't home yet" Narissa replied.

"Has he called?" Kim asked worried.

"Nah" Narissa said with heavy chested sigh.

Kim looked at her with eyebrows squinting. "Aren't you mad? How dare he stand you up like this?"

"I hope he is just running late, caught up while doing something nice for me like buying flowers." Deep down in her heart, Narissa knew it wasn't true. Lawrence can never think of anyone accept for himself and people around him.

What you cannot see doesn't exist and who is not with you doesn't matter. This is Lawrence's way. Narissa was feeling gutted inside and there was no way she was going to show her inner turmoil to Kim or the kids.

7.45pm and she started breaking out in a sweat. She was anxious. This has happened to her before but she always remained positive. Kim can tell that was disappointed and she says, "I think you should eat."

Narissa cannot ever remember having this kind of feeling in her life, not even for her university exams. She cannot understand why and how she turned out to be this way.

Narissa always waited for Lawrence to come home and eat together, even when he gave her the silent treatment. Even when she was pregnant with the children and her stomach would rumble, she always waited for Lawrence to come home and eat while he off loaded his work problems. After living with Lawrence for so long she knew his needs and she responded to them in an appropriate manner.

Lawrence wanted her to wait for her and got really wild when Narissa had eaten without him once while pregnant with Maddie because she couldn't hold her hunger any longer. When he came home he gave her the third degree. He told her she was selfish. "I have already eaten because I couldn't wait and it is not good to wait especially when you are pregnant" Narissa had told him.

Lawrence's reaction took Narissa by surprise. She hadn't expected him to give her such a displeasing, maddening words. "So now you go eating on your own as if I don't exist."

Hold it, he comes home at 9pm and expects a pregnant woman to wait for 5 hours for dinner? Surely he doesn't mean that.

That happened again. He was late from work, maybe 8.30pm or 9pm and Narissa had just eaten when he arrived home. "Honey I have eaten already."

"You are making a habit of this!" He exclaimed.

"You expect me to wait for you? You told me you will be home at 6 and it is now 9 o'clock and I am supposed to wait?" Narissa shrieked.

"Are you out of your mind?"

Narissa had been very cautious about eating on her own. Usually she fed the children, cleaned and tidied up the kitchen and if by then there was still no sign of Lawrence she might eat. She was usually starving by 7 o'clock. After that her hunger disappeared. Lawrence didn't understand nor did he care. Even when Narissa was breastfeeding, she used to get so thirsty and sometimes really hungry. She ate fruit or had glass of milk which she got told off many times for the fruit finishing and not enough milk for his cereal in the morning.

Narissa really didn't understand Lawrence at all. "I just bought fruit last Sunday and you guys have already finished it all! What happens to the milk in this house? Have you guys got any respect! I earn and you all live off me" he used to say.

Wow! What has respect got to do with that? Fruit may last a week and milk may last 3-4 days. 'What does he think I do?' Narissa thought.

She was very careful about spending. She cooked every day and baked whatever she could. She bought all bulk and raw ingredients to cook at home. It's not just healthy, it is a lot cheaper too. 'What on earth is he going on about' she thought.

It is now 8.30pm and Kim reckons she can go home. Narissa paid Kim cash but today she refused the money. She feels bad and sad for Narissa. She wants to stay a bit longer because she thinks she has a right to say something to Lawrence.

8.45pm and Kim and Narissa heard his car pull up the driveway. Kim came up "what are you going to say?"

Narissa didn't know how to answer that. She had mixed feelings and felt pretty rotten. She didn't feel like talking to him but at the same time she was a very patient person and always felt that people don't hurt others knowingly.

"Oh hi." Lawrence is very polite and smiles seeing Kim there with Narissa. "How are you, Kim? Good to see you. How's school going?"

Kim is dying to ask him if he is planning on going out. Narissa could see her restless hands as she was clicking her fingers, perched on the side arm of the sofa, legs swinging around.

"It IS Valentine's Day today and you had a date with your wife" Kim exclaimed.

What Kim doesn't know is that Lawrence doesn't give a hoot as to what day it was. He was the biggest pretender you will find. He looked at the clock "gosh! I totally forgot!" Lawrence said it with a smirk on his face, treating Narissa like a little child.

"Forgot!" Narissa couldn't help herself.

"I sent you messages 3 times today, and called and left messages too" she carried on in a calmer voice.

"I didn't check my messages" he replied.

'Really? How many times have I heard that one?' Narissa thought.

"Why do you think Kim is here today? She looked at him suggestively. "I told you I had got the babysitting organised today."

"So that means we can't go anymore, right? It is quite late now isn't it?" He casually replied.

Narissa absolutely hates it when he does that. He looks down at her and pretends that it is not a big deal at all. His eyes dart around like he is looking for more excuses.

"Where are the flowers?" Kim is not feeling good at all. She goes on to say "she hasn't eaten yet either, you know."

"Really?" He replied.

'Yes, really because if I do then I get told off' Narissa thought to herself.

"Shall we eat then?" He replied.

"Kim, would you like me to drop you off home?" Lawrence offered very politely. He always offers young girls and looks after the pretty ones.

"It's ok. Mum is on her way." Lucky Kim lives down the road from us. Her mum must be wondering why Kim wanted to be picked up so early.

Narissa went to the kitchen to dish dinner out. Kim came from behind her and laid her soft gentle hands on her shoulders, "you ok?"

With a smile on her face and with a voice full of confidence Narissa just replied "yeah, I am good."

'What can a sixteen year old say. I bet this is off putting for her. She won't like to be with a guy like this.' Narissa thought.

"I hope he has got some surprise for you." Kim manages a smile.

The most annoying part is that Lawrence hasn't even noticed that Narissa was all dressed up. Can't he even take the initiative and suggest something, like going out for a dessert or drinks since Kim was here. He cannot take advantage of life at all.

"Oh well, we can watch a movie at home."

They sat down to eat and Lawrence starts gulping his food down. Mouthfuls of rice is disappearing and he doesn't even stop to talk, let alone breath.

"Seriously, tell me that you didn't plan to go out tonight, did you?

You ignored my messages purposely, didn't you?" Narissa asked angrily.

She was still eating and Lawrence left the table rudely. Then he made himself comfortable on the sofa in the lounge and opened his computer. He started checking his emails and then Narissa heard him chatting to one of his colleagues, like a skype call but without pictures.

"So what are you doing with your Valentine today?" asks Russell.

"Haha, Well I am sitting at home with a glass of wine and watching movie with my Valentine" he replied laughingly.

"You can't be, because you are chatting with me, mate. I will let you go, man" he replied.

Firstly, it is all a lie. She was sitting on the sofa next to him but there is no wine and there is no movie. She looked at him with sharp eyes and thinking what a prick.

Not worth sitting here and playing the good housewife.

In the bathroom as she was removing her makeup, she thought of the guy at the cafe. 'Was there a message for me? Clearly, my husband has no interest in me. He didn't ask about my day and didn't bother asking about the children, didn't bother admiring my look and appreciating all the effort I made today.

There are no chocolates or flowers. All I got was cold shoulders, again!' Narissa thought with her heart aching and tears building up.

After cleaning the kitchen and preparing for next day she slipped into her pyjamas and thought she will never set herself up for disappointment again.

She was falling asleep feeling very empty inside.

"Sometimes we expect more from others because we will be willing to do that much for them."—

# CHAPTER 16

*"Give the ones you love wings to fly, roots to come*
*back, and reasons to stay."* —Dalai Lama

H ER NEIGHBOUR CAME up and asked Narissa if her children would like to go the park with his three children. Tim is so helpful. Amanda, his beautiful wife loves children and she is a brilliant cook as well. Amanda makes the most amazing soups and cakes. Narissa's children could live at her house. Amanda knows that Narissa is very busy with three children as she has three of her own, similar ages to Narissa's and they get on well together. The only difference is Amanda has a husband who is very helpful. Sometimes she sees Tim taking the rubbish out at night when Narissa is taking hers out or cleaning the car with his children. He also cooks once a week and cleans the house and gets the washing in. Tim always asks Amanda if she needs help. Tim takes the kids down to the parks on Saturday morning so Amanda can clean the bathrooms and wash the floor. By the time her family returns from their outing she has done all that and put on a nice lunch.

Rubbish day is Wednesday morning and Narissa puts it out at night around 10.30 or 11 before she has her shower and gets ready for bed. The recycling bin is an open container and Narissa has to make sure that rubbish stays down and not flies around. Some nights it is so cold that she dreads going out but someone has to take the rubbish out. Tonight is a cold blistery night and she was not looking forward to going out. Regardless, she braved it and went outside as she didn't have a choice. Down the path to put the rubbish bins on the kerb. She felt someone behind her and it wasn't the children as they were all in the house alone. Narissa immediately turned around, palms in a fist ready to hit them and realised it just her neighbour from across the road. It is dark but the angle he is standing at has street light shining on him. "Oh hi Rob. You scared the daylights out of me." Narissa picked up the courage to speak.

"What are you doing in this rain?" "Where's Lawrence? He should be doing this for you?" Rob replied.

"Ha, he has a fairy in the house and things happen magically" she said laughingly. "Anyway, good night."

Narissa has asked Lawrence several times but he won't listen. Fed up of asking she just pushes herself to get things done, despite rain hail or shine.

Today is a beautiful Saturday morning and she was putting clothes on the line. Max came running down the side of the house towards Narissa at the clothesline. "Mum, can I please go to the park with Hamish?" "I will be good. I promise."

"Let me speak with Tim first" Narissa replied.

"He said he will take me, mum" Max replied very enthusiastically. "Please. Please mum" he begged her.

Just then Tim appeared "Where is Lawrence? Is he working?" asked Tim.

"No, he is in bed. As you know, his day starts at 12pm on a weekend." Narissa replied sadly to Tim.

Tim just looked at her like was a silly woman for putting up with his crap.

"It is such a beautiful day," said Tim and walked away.

Narissa's dad used to say, people who sleep in, lose part of their life. Obviously Lawrence didn't get these life lessons.

What amazed Narissa was that Lawrence would never get up

early to take the children to the park, swimming lessons or even to their sports, but he will if he was coaching or had a breakfast meeting at work or catch a plane for work. His priority was never the kids or his wife.

Both Ella and Max were playing soccer in nursery grade. Narissa put them in the same team because it saved her running to too many different grounds. Maddie had her netball and that was enough for Narissa to handle on a Saturday morning.

Lawrence volunteered to coach Ella and Max's team together with another mother. Lawrence loves the praises he receives from all the mothers. He is a charmer and stays calm and involved with the children. He put in so much effort. Every Friday he would sit and map out the players and think of all the drills and got really excited.

What really surprised Narissa was that he was never like this with his children at home? At the soccer training, which was once a week he will get out to the grounds early, leaving work early with his gear ready. Occasionally he had forgotten his training bag or soccer balls. Narissa would get a phone call to drop off his bag and balls to the grounds. It was such a hassle for her because she felt that's the time she could use effectively preparing dinner or getting more work done around the house without much disturbance. She always had something to do and by having to pick up things for Lawrence, dropping them off when she had already dropped the children at the ground wastes so much of her time.

Lawrence didn't care. He would shrug his shoulders as if nothing mattered. What got Narissa was that this is not just a once off or second time thing. This was most weeks.

One thing she learnt was to look for Lawrence's bag before he left home. Despite Narissa reminding him of all his activities, he would forget.

Surely, he would have learnt his lesson by now.

Narissa learnt that he thought too much about himself, how people will see him and he frets about the skills he teaches these kids, he goes over and over little drills in his head and gets totally stressed.

He would spend entire Saturday and Friday night over thinking the drills for soccer. Sometimes, to the point where everyone around him irritated him. Those days, Narissa would have to get the kids out of the house to avoid verbal abuse or someone being hurt.

Yet, if Lawrence was sent to a park with the children, he couldn't do it.

One Sunday morning when soccer season was all over and kids were a bit restless, she asked Lawrence if he would like to take kids to the park. "Honey, I think the kids would love to go down to the park and kick a ball around." Max has come upstairs with his ball. He is really happy and you can see the glittering eyes like precious diamonds and the smile that just melts your heart.

"Get that filthy ball out of here!" Shrieked Lawrence.

"D-ad, can we go to the park, please please Dad." Max is begging Lawrence.

"Get this ball outside! You know the rules! No balls in the house! You stupid boy" Lawrence screamed at Max and almost ready to throw something at him.

Lawrence has no parenting skills at all. He screams and yells and carries on, churning out hurtful words. Narissa got angry with him. Usually she is quiet but she learnt that the children will grow up thinking that this sort of hurtful words were acceptable. Now she sometimes intervenes to make Lawrence understand that he needs to learn to talk nicely to the children.

At soccer, he doesn't talk to the children like this at all. He will speak to everyone politely even if the kids are really misbehaving. He goes down to his knees and shows other mums that he is a charming man. He smiles, speaks softly and pats them on shoulders as if they are little gems.

Most mums at soccer comment on how wonderful Lawrence is with the children. 'If only they knew the real him' thought Narissa.

It is 3 o'clock in the afternoon and Max had waited a long time to go to the park. He asks again "but Dad you said soon before. We have had lunch and you still not going." "Will we ever go?" Max speaks out in a pouty voice.

"Max, I am busy. Can't you see?" Lawrence screams out. "These kids are so demanding! Don't you teach them anything? What kind of a mother are you?" he carried on.

Wow, hello. "Did I promise to take them to the park?" "Did I say, yeah soon?"

"Lawrence, you said you were taking them to the park this morning, didn't you?" "Well?"

'What kind of a mother am I? Seriously? Demanding kids?' fuck him she thought.

4 o'clock and kids are still waiting. Ella had dressed herself in some warm clothes with her barrette as well. Maddie had water bottles sitting by the front door. Both Ella and Maddie had been asking Lawrence if he was planning on leaving soon.

Narissa couldn't take them right now. She has to prepare for the next day, think about the morning rush and get the clothes off the line and do some ironing, prepare dinner as well.

It is now 4.30 and Maddie is getting stroppy. "It isn't fair. I could have gone with Phoebe and her family. Dad said he was taking us to the park!"

Ella comes up "Mumma is dad taking us? Can you take us instead?"

Narissa is very patient and if she had known that this was going to fall on her lap as well she would have taken the children ages ago. She thought for a second, then made a snap decision and excitedly said "yes let's go."

The cheers and excitement from all three children was enough to lift her spirits up. It made her happy. "Where's dad?" she asked.

"Dunno," Maddie replies in her usual cute tone.

Narissa looked around for Lawrence and found him sitting and reading his paper. "Hey, I am taking the children to the park. Are you able to put dinner on? I have drumsticks all marinated, just chuck them in the oven. Everything is ready and you just have to put it all in the oven. I will do the vegetables when I come home or you can if you have time" Narissa called out.

"I was going to take them but they are so impatient!" he yelled.

'Impatient? They have waited since 10 this morning and it is now 4.45pm. Is that being impatient?' thought Narissa.

"They have waited all day Lawrence. They could have gone with Phoebe's family but you stopped them. That's disappointing, isn't it?" she said.

Who is being irresponsible?

No point arguing with someone who just doesn't get it. It just means more work for Narissa as it is she works hard all day, every hour from the moment she wakes up to the time she goes to bed, seven days a week.

At the park they kicked a ball around and Ella went on her favourite item, the climbing frame and Maddie her swing, even though they had a swing set at home.

Lawrence hated it when Narissa bought the swing and the sliding set for home. Her argument was that the kids needed to have their exercise and she couldn't take them to the park everyday plus they lived in a house with a small yard with not enough room to run around. All the friends absolutely loved the swings, the slide and the trampoline.

They were very happy dribbling the ball around when another family joined in. The two boys must have been around four or five. Their father decided to make goal posts and they found ourselves in a team. It was them against us. They were dribbling and passing the ball around and in the midst of all this Narissa became the goal keeper for their team and the other father became the goal keeper for his team. How we slotted into these roles, no one ever knew, but they were cheering for their own children to pass to each other and score.

The goal keeper's role was a bit sublime compared to all the running Narissa had to do passing the ball around. Both parents, Narissa and this other guy were puffed from running around. It was so fun and suddenly Narissa realised that she had lost track of time.

"Hey, we have to go soon, guys" Narissa told everyone.

The other guy, whose name she didn't know nor bothered asking because they had just met and what are the chances they will meet again? Probably never. So names didn't matter. One of the boys wasn't happy at all. He wanted Narissa and the kids to stay, "but we just started" he claimed.

With a smile Narissa kneeled down to the level of the boys, "I am so sorry, but I have to go home cook dinner and get ready for school tomorrow." Then she go up and turned to the father, "You guys must have to go soon too, huh?"

Their father left his goal keeping position and came up, turned around "Yeah, we will be going soon. School night, boys. Remember what mum said...don't be too long."

With a smile he turned to his boys and said "I am sorry guys we must get going soon."

Narissa thought about it for a second and in her head she was thinking 'I hope Lawrence has put the dinner in the oven and then we can stay a bit longer.'

The father of the boys had been curious "so you are on your own, huh?"

"Well, not exactly. I have an absent husband. The kind that is present physically but absent emotionally" Narissa replied with regrettably.

"What a shame," he said. "He is missing out on life."

Few more minutes and they were on their way back home. Maddie and Max would have loved to stay longer. Trust Maddie to come up with the idea of staying behind and innocently suggesting that they can all come home in this strange man's car.

Sometimes Maddie is too trusting. Narissa had explained to her so many times and reinstated the view that she should never accept sweets, rides or any offers from any strangers. "But they were so nice!" Maddie says very innocently.

"Only for that moment, Maddie. You can never trust anyone" Narissa explained.

They reached home, one by one out of the car. Narissa got the kids put the balls away, shoes put into their proper place and then get to the showers. She went in the kitchen and was so disappointed. The dinner was still in the fridge. She was mad but at the same time she should have known better. It is nearly six o'clock. This is normally when kids have dinner. "Lawrence! What is this?" She exclaims.

He doesn't move. He is still reading the paper. Narissa's anger is rising but she was trying to hold it in.

"Lawrence, do you know what time this is? I just asked you to put everything in the oven" she screams at him.

She always made sure that when she tells Lawrence to do something she has his full attention and that he acknowledges it.

"Oh, I didn't know what time I had to put it in" he replied.

'What a crap excuse! Is that the best he can come up with' she thought.

"You know that kids eat at 6 every night and if I don't feed them now they will eat late, sleep late and then I am stuffed in the morning!" She can't help herself. She is hyperventilating and feeling that her world will collapse. The disappointment she has experienced all her life with this irresponsible man is just too much. He is childlike.

For the sake of the children Narissa was trying to hold it in.

Ella walks in "Mumma, I am hungry." Behind her is Maddie, "Mumma, did dad cook today? What is it?"

I have to say Maddie is always so hopeful. I cuddle them both and said "sorry darlings, daddy didn't cook."

"We can have some fruit and water and then we will shower. By that stage dinner should be ready.

"Oh sorry mumma. We should have left earlier, shouldn't we?" Maddie says with great disappointment.

"No Maddie, not your fault" Narissa explained.

"Daddy doesn't care! Does he mumma" Maddie says.

'He thinks he is living at home with his mother. For fuck's

sakes...you are somebody's husband and a father, grow up! That's what I really want to say.'

As she cut the fruit for the children, Lawrence enters the kitchen. "Why are you eating fruit now? Isn't it dinner time?"

"Do you see your mother here cooking for me?" Narissa's anger is rising.

She banged the casserole dish out of the fridge and chucked it into the cold oven, she forgot to put it on before. She transferred the potatoes out of the bowl with water and chucked them into a pan to boil. Might be easier to do mashed potatoes instead. She had to chop the broccoli, cauliflower and carrots and put them in the pot too.

In all this time Lawrence just stood there, not even offering to help.

The girls have finished their fruit but Maddie is looking for something else to eat. Narissa gave her a pot of yoghurt and Ella wants one too. She had a horrible feeling that this will be their dinner tonight. Someone will wake up hungry.

Max wants to be fed too. He has a few pieces of fruit but Max wants solid food. "Mumma, when is dinner ready?" he calls out with dismay.

"Well, if you hadn't insisted on going to the park, you would have had dinner!" Lawrence screamed.

How could Lawrence be so insensitive? Why can't he think that if he had put dinner on then his family would have had dinner when they came home?

Everyone else has a normal family, normal life.

Narissa had a brilliant thought... "why don't I put the bath on and you can all go in the bath."

She knows that Lawrence won't keep an eye on the oven and he won't bathe the kids either.

"Lawrence, do you think you can shower the children?"

"Yup" he replies without thinking. That's what Narissa usually gets. Just yup but no action. Time is not an issue for Lawrence. He couldn't care less. As long as his clothes are washed and he has food, life is sweet.

He has not offered to help in all this time. Narissa was running to the shower but she realised that the kids were older now and she cannot put them all in the bath together. 'However, if I put one then they will all want to be in it. I am just trying to buy myself some time' she was thinking.

She got Maddie in the shower, since Lawrence has disappeared again. While Maddie is showering, Narissa was back in the kitchen watching and getting table set out. She can hear someone screaming. She ran down the hallway "What is it?" She screamed.

Lawrence is in the bathroom, pulling Maddie out. He has his grip on Maddie's forearm.

Narissa held Lawrence's arm "what are you doing? I just put her in the shower!" Maddie knows when to come out. Maddie is beginning to scream and beat the shower floor with her feet.

She is screaming "Daddy don't hurt me!"

Narissa can't take it anymore. She swung her arm around and hit Lawrence on his back "leave her alone!"

She pushed him out of the bathroom. All her suppressed anger is now pouring out. "You don't want to help, you can't play with your children and yet you are ready to abuse. Get out of here!" she shouted.

Oh the neighbours would have heard. She let Maddie clean herself as she could see Maddie still had soap on her back. Couldn't Lawrence see that?

Narissa thought she should have just got baked beans and poached eggs on toast for dinner today. She was half crying without tears but sighs and gulps are finding its way out of her body.

For Lawrence, baked beans wouldn't do. He wants a good home cooked meal and yet not prepared to help.

Sometimes, Narissa wonders why she bothers. If only she had a full time job, was able to support her children she would have left.

Lawrence was brought up by a stay-at-home mum and he doesn't want anything different in his home. Maybe he thinks it is a woman's job to stay at home and raise kids and look after him. When Narissa asked him his view on this his answer was no way. He didn't think he needed looking after. He was earning and supporting a family, what more could anyone possibly need.

If that's the case, he should really be providing for them and not complaining on her spending. As it is Narissa is very conservative when she shops for groceries, she doesn't waste water, electricity or gas. She doesn't buy clothes or shoes every day, she doesn't go out. She hasn't shopped for clothes for herself in years. She simply can't afford them since she stopped working. She doesn't go out with friends even if she gets invited.

Lawrence can't provide for them all and yet won't help out so Narissa could have a part time job. She is stuck in a limbo.

Narissa spoke to him regarding getting a nanny on a part time basis or a cleaner. The anger associated with that was horrible. "You go and find money to pay for it all!" The tone he uses is so degrading. 'If I worked, I will have money to pay for a nanny or a cleaner.' Narissa had thought.

Narissa couldn't go part-time teaching and she couldn't go and work as a relief teacher because that will mean getting a baby sitter quickly. She also let her registration lapse.

Then one day she saw a brilliant course, training to be a Beauty therapist. Walla! This was an 18 month course and after graduating she could practice from her own home. 'Brilliant! I can set up the room downstairs and work from home. Perfect!' she thought.

Narissa enrolled and it was a real easy process. She had done a Certificate in Business management and could study weekends and some evenings. 'OMG! I am so excited. I would pamper my girls when they grow older. I can just see them in their teenage years wanting waxing done, make up and getting their friends over for girlie parties. 'I can totally see myself with this business' Narissa thought with excitement.

She told Lawrence that the classes were held in the evening and some weekends and she should be able to manage. He didn't say anything at all so Narissa went ahead. It was a struggle for her but she managed. She had friends and neighbours who chipped in.

Narissa got a part time nanny but Lawrence complained about the funds. Narissa became a heartless but strong woman and she was determined to get this done.

After 18 months of a lot of juggling, she graduated. Happiest moment of her life. Lawrence didn't go to her graduation. Narissa only stayed for the first part and left before dinner. She will soon be doing something more meaningful with her life. 'Finally have some adult conversation' she thought.

In her enthusiasm, she got the downstairs room all set up and ready for her first client. She was nervous but excited at the same time. Narissa had a table and some trolleys and all her equipment and she painted the room herself with the colours she loved. Maddie was too eager to help and she was horrified when Ella took the brush and painted the wrong spot.

The deep mauve colour of her room was so soothing and the artificial white magnolia with chocolate stem in a white vase was just so appealing. The candles on the shelves and her oil burner, perfect! She used the old paint left over from Maddie and Ella's rooms and mixed them together. She got a table as part of her course and she had found some towels that hadn't been used before. She bought them in a sale but they were too small for them to use on a daily basis.

She had her very first client at home and spent 2 hours when it should have taken her an hour but Narissa took it as a good experience. She can always change and build as she grows with this venture. Lawrence was at work and kids at school, she can work the hours she wanted. She was able to pick kids from school, take them to sport and prepare all the meals. Being her own boss allowed her the flexible lifestyle to feed the family's needs. Above all it allowed Lawrence to have his freedom to lead his own life.

That night she told Lawrence excitedly "I had my first client today, here at home."

He glanced at her, squinting his eyes in anger and said "I don't want strangers coming to my house."

"Sorry, I thought you were happy for me to work from home.

You have changed your mind?" Narissa is really surprised at his comment.

"I don't want people coming home!" he exclaims like this is not a discussion. It is his decision and Narissa has to follow.

"I have already got some flyers out and put the word out there. You had agreed to this before!" Narissa responded angrily.

She can't believe what she is hearing.

"I have seen your flyer. Why do you have to use your name?" he replies sternly.

"What do you mean? I haven't come up with a name for the business and thought I will just use my name for now" she explained.

In fact Narissa wanted to put her picture on the flyer as well Lawrence didn't take any pictures of her. Every time Narissa asked him he was busy. He never had time for her anyway.

The printer was not the best so the flyer looked very unprofessional but 'once I have a few clients, I should be able to afford a better printer' she thought with sadness.

That is another thing. When it comes to buying electronics, Lawrence thinks he knows best. He won't let Narissa have an input in deciding on what sort of computer they can buy, camera or printer. He knows best and yet he does the wrong thing. This printer he bought was useless. The ink runs out very quickly and the printing was very faded.

Narissa had to get this printer in a hurry because she was disgusted at Lawrence for holding her back for too long.

One Parent teacher interview, this teacher showed Narissa Maddie's poster which hand was written, cut out and stuck on cardboard. Narissa remembers doing it with Maddie. The teacher showed Narissa rest of the class's poster and they were all printed material. He said the kids are expected to produce printed material like these. Narissa didn't tell the teacher that they didn't have a computer and didn't have a printer. She just apologised as she was feeling a bit embarrassed. The teacher added that Maddie could print at the school if there was a problem.

Narissa didn't have a computer at home so how could Maddie take her stick to print at school.

Narissa asked Maddie later at home and she had said that she got tired of asking dad and decided to hand write. "So what did you tell your teacher?" Narissa asked.

"I told them that our printer was broken." Gosh, Maddie is beginning to lie as well. 'I have become a liar and making my kids into liars as well' thought Narissa.

Her heart bled for Maddie.

This is one time Narissa really got into Lawrence. She told him her disgust at his lack of support. "When Maddie had been asking for a use of a computer, you said you will look into it! When she asked for a printer, you said she didn't need one! The school showed me her work, hand written work! The teacher tells me she lost marks because it is not typed! Do you care? Do you give a damn about your children?" Narissa asked angrily.

"I don't have funds to go out and buy a computer or a printer." Lawrence comes up with the most pathetic excuses.

This is why Narissa wanted to work from home.

She had gone out and bought a computer for Maddie and then Lawrence picked up a printer from his work that was being thrown out. She only discovered this later, that it was a rejected printer from work. She only found out about it because it won't print colour properly and she was looking for the booklet for troubleshoot. It took a while like many days before Lawrence admitted that he didn't have the booklet as it was a rejected printer from work.

Therefore, after all these dramas and lack of support, she decided working from home was a good option for her so she could keep sanity and her children happy.

The next day, Narissa went into her studio to just admire her beautiful created space and she freaked out. She couldn't believe it. She was breaking out in sobs.

Someone, she is thinking, Lawrence had moved her bed to a side, moved all her candles from the shelves and put his books, and he had re arranged the table and Narissa couldn't handle it any longer. She was spewing...where did her towels go? She exasperated. She was breaking out in a sweat. All her hard work had been undone. 'How could he move M-Y stuff around without asking?' She thought.

That's Lawrence for you. He will move your stuff because he feels it is his right over everything he has paid for. It sounds crazy but over the years Narissa has learnt that that's how he feels. He will barge into the children's room like it is his. If they argue about something he tells them that he has paid for it and that they should leave.

Cleaning up mass, oh oh hell no. If it's not Lawrence's then forget it. Narissa cleans the garage, cleans the kitchen, all the window sills, the glass doors, picture frames, the back yard, the patio, the front yard and it is all because it isn't Lawrence's mass.

She was furious! 'How dare he do this to me? I am trying to make a living the best way I can and he ruins it for me? Wait, my certificate is missing too' Narissa is now noticing everything in the room.

She can't bear this. She called him at work. It goes straight to his answer phone. She kept ringing his phone and then he answered, whispering "I can't talk right now. I will call you in a second."

She waited for an hour and he didn't call back. Narissa began re arranging her room. He can't do this! She is sobbing and kicking his books and the desk. "He can't be such an arsehole."

Narissa has to move so much and with exasperated sobs her energy is being burnt and she was feeling hyperventilated.

Just then her phone rings and she quickly took some deep breaths, like real deep ones to calm herself down as quickly as possible just in case it is a possible client.

"Good afternoon, Narissa's beauty clinic. How can I help you" Narissa answered in a polite voice. She could see the caller number was unfamiliar so she changed her tone and tune of her voice.

"Oh Hi. I got your number from a friend of mine and I live in your area. I was wondering if I could make an appointment for this afternoon, like before school pick up." She sounded very young and must be a young mother. Narissa took all the details of the treatment she was after and she put it all on a card so that when her customer arrived she wouldn't have to ask her again. Narissa really wanted this business to go well. She wanted to be a real professional. Suddenly, she was very excited. She had forgotten Lawrence taking over her space. 'I am ME now and I want to work this' she said to herself.

"Sure, I can see you around 1.30 today and you should be finished by 2.30. Will that give you enough time to pick up kids?" Narissa asked.

Suddenly Narissa was feeling really good about herself. She felt useful as she was looking around her room absorbing some positive energy around herself, infiltrating her body with this slightly inflated mood.

"That will be perfect! I look forward to meeting you. My friend said, you are really good." She sounds charming, Narissa thought.

Narissa got moving at the speed of lightening, getting her room organised, running upstairs to have a quick lunch and be super ready for her second client this week. She had forgotten about the call from Lawrence and at this stage she didn't feel the need to talk to him at all now.

Lawrence has a habit of not answering his phone when Narissa calls him. So one day while looking for the printer manual, she came across the manual for the home phone. She learnt how to make a call with blocked caller ID. She had caught Lawrence a few times. He won't answer her call but when she calls him with the caller ID blocked he answers. He will ask her if she had tried calling him before and her answer was "yes" and he will come up with an excuse. Sometimes she say "No" and he will say "Oh it's just that I was away from my desk." One thing with Narissa is that she cannot tell a lie. She knows that a lie once will come back to haunt you one day. That's what her mum used to say when she was a kid. She sometimes did lie to mum, little white lies but mum could tell, somehow. So Narissa learnt to respect her mum on that one.

Narissa didn't like hurting anyone even with her words. Usually she tried to keep her angry words to myself. For Narissa

Shabina

the angry words are like hitting someone with something hard and it can make dents in the other person like dents in cars when a stone is thrown on it.

'If Lawrence comes home and rearranges my room, I will be mad! I will kick him out today! I will leave him today! I will not tolerate this anymore!' she thought angrily.

"A real man sees beyond your physical realm and understands the kind of support you need to sail through and gives it all to you."

# CHAPTER 17

*"It is vital that when educating our children's brains that we do not neglect to educate their hearts."* —Dalai Lama

MADDIE IS NOW 22 and absolutely hates her father to the point where she would like to dissociate herself from her father and change her surname. Max turned 19 and he doesn't know who his father really is, Ella is turning 17 this year and has no interest in her family. She is a social butterfly and loves being out with friends all the time. I think that is her escape route.

Maddie is at University studying very hard. After so many years of fighting with her father, she has decided that he is not worth the effort, instead she does her own thing and lets him yell at her. She manages to block it off. She is very devoted to her studies and doesn't seem too interested in boyfriends right now. After being verbally abused for so long, Narissa can understand that Maddie doesn't trust men at all. She has a few men interested in her but she pushes them away. She has been to coffees but refuses to go to movies or dinners. She treads very cautiously around men. She spends most of her time at home in her room on her computer watching movies, reading books or knitting. She has some close friends but everyone seems to be busy these days. Maddie and Narissa catch up on coffee dates and it is nice to have a daughter who isn't shy to be seen with her mother.

Narissa often wonders if it was her fault for staying with Lawrence in this marriage but at the same time she felt sorry for him and couldn't leave him in the state he was in.

Lawrence needed help with everyday mechanics of life which Narissa realised a long time ago but it only took her 20 years to learn about his difficulties with life, with people, with time and boundaries.

Max has a girlfriend who is the nicest person you will meet in life. She is a rare find. She absolutely adores Max. Both Max's sisters love her too. The only person that has problems with everything anyone does in the house, is Lawrence.

Max and Zoe are at the same university but taking different Degrees. Yet, Zoe finds time to visit Max at home whenever he has a day off from work or studies. Ella is very studious as well. Narissa is so glad that both girls have decided to take on this academic pathway. She certainly wants the best for them, to discover their own world first before they go out into the big wide world.

Sometimes Ella gets distracted. She can be a wild thing. At 17 she has more friends than Maddie or Max but at the same time it is hard to tell if she has any friends that she has deep connections with. She can seem a bit aloof, but at the same time she is very cautious with boys.

Ella doesn't have as much respect for Narissa as Maddie does, but Narissa has herself to blame. Ella has seen enough dramas and Narissa crying and feeling down. She has often questioned Narissa why she didn't leave Lawrence earlier.

"Clearly Ma, dad is a real selfish prick and he is very mean sometimes too. He has no respect for you. What I don't understand is why have you put up with this for so long?" Ella asks Narissa while folding clothes. Girls have started washing their own clothes and all because Narissa used to mix up all the socks and undies. Ella was folding clothes so Narissa decided to go into her room and have a chat about her university work and answering her million questions.

Narissa thinks to herself how mature she is.

"I don't know, Ella" Narissa replied sighing.

Sitting on the edge of her bed, Narissa looked at her and replied, "perhaps, I have been wondering how I was going to support you all. I couldn't work full time and be there for you all at the same time".

Ella just nods her head. "People d-o marry the wrong people, you know." She gives a little smile.

'Gosh, she is so right. I wish I had her intelligence when I realised how difficult my marriage was. I was scared of raising three children on my own and I was of the impression that children needed their fathers too. I guess I stayed because of the children but there was no way I can say this to Ella. I definitely don't want her to live with guilt' Narissa thought deeply.

She was not Lawrence. He always made people feel guilty and useless, but only at home. At work he was the Prince charming, pleasing every woman in the office, pleasing every customer at work. He would yell at the family for getting a dog yet he will brag to people how beautiful his dog is. He would scream at Maddie playing her music, yet he will show off his music to his friends on his iPad or phone.

Max has no interest in anything in life. He floats around friends, school and it is a wonder that he has made it to University. He had several difficulties at school, chopping and changing subjects, and didn't know what he wanted to do. It is a pity that he was such a bright young boy but no real mentor at home or school. With all the arguments at home, his energy was always low, so was Ella's, Maddie's and Narissa's, in fact the whole family's except Lawrence's.

Max loved hanging out with his friends Fathers much to Lawrence's disappointment. Lawrence gets very jealous when Max goes out fishing or camping with his friend's dads. Lawrence would never think of doing it himself and whenever Max goes out he gets really wound up.

Max always acted tough and like a grown man but deep inside Narissa knew he wants love from his father. Lawrence doesn't think much of his children. He has told Narissa enough times that she has spoilt them, given them too much love, not helped them to have respect for their father and basically have raised very ungrateful children.

This view is not held by Narissa's friends who think she has raised extremely balanced children. They have seen the children with Narissa more than with Lawrence and if they see the dynamics with Lawrence, their view may change.

Zoe seems to have a lot of interest in Max, making plans to do things together, going for long drives, movies, trampolining and Max just tags along. Narissa has been the father for him when he was growing up. He used to go out into the garden and Max would help Narissa with the digging and driving the wheelbarrow. He loved cars, electronics, tools and was a boisterous boy. When he was 10 Narissa bought him a remote controlled car which took petrol and was a real buzz. This car couldn't be taken onto dirt and Max told Lawrence exactly what the lady at the shop told him. Lawrence never took children's advice. It was always his way. The one and only time Lawrence took hold of that controller, he drove the car into dirt, broke the clutch and never replaced it. Max asked him 50 times if he was going to replace it, but Lawrence wouldn't. I wanted to but Lawrence takes offence if Narissa got involved. For Lawrence everything is a competition and there is one winner, HIM.

Lawrence comes up with pathetic excuses, example, it was a cheap version; the car should have had a better clutch; Narissa should have consulted him before buying etc. Just because Max and Narissa had bought the car, Lawrence was very jealous. Narissa explained to Lawrence that it had a plastic clutch and they were told that when Max has had good grasp of the mechanics and learnt about the parts and their functions, then they could replace the clutch and other parts with metal ones as required, but no, Lawrence had to spoil it for him. She suggested to Lawrence that he could replace the clutch and in that way he can make connections with his son. He can get more involved with Max. Instead, Lawrence told her that the clutch was too expensive to replace and that he was going to find a better car, which after five years, didn't happen.

Just like bike riding. Narissa always took the children for bike rides. One day, Lawrence decided to take Max for a bike ride when Max was five. He took him on a 15Km bike ride. Max had never been riding that far and his bike didn't have gears. It was a kid's bike. Max was exhausted, furious and apparently Lawrence was trying to race with him. Lawrence, obviously had a top notch bike with gears, a comfortable seat and handles.

When they came back, Max said his legs were killing him. He was crying and said "Dad is mean and cruel! I am never ever going for a bike ride with him! Never ever in my life!"

Narissa didn't understand at that time and asked Lawrence what had happened. He just shut his mouth. Narissa has to ask fifty times before he will give one version, then it may change and he will continue to lie. Lawrence blamed Narissa for listening to the children. "Well, why would Max scream in pain?" She asked.

According to Lawrence, the kids were trying to make Lawrence look like a bad father.

'I give up,' thought Narissa.

Narissa learnt about it years later how Lawrence tortured Max. Max told her when he was around 11. She glanced at Lawrence but Lawrence didn't say a word. It meant it was true. He was hiding the truth for so long. How can anyone live with such a conscience?

At night when all the kids were fast asleep, Narissa asked Lawrence "is it true what Max said this afternoon?"

"What about?" Lawrence asked as if he didn't know what she was asking him about.

"The 15km bike ride and how you pushed Max. No wonder his legs had become so hard and red that day. He couldn't play soccer and had complained of sore legs" she said to Lawrence.

Lawrence didn't answer for a while. Then suddenly Lawrence splurges out "when I was his age, I rode my bike everywhere. What kind of a boy is he? A pussy!"

"Wow, I am gobsmacked!" Narissa said

"What kind of bike did you have? With gears? Did you ride a lot every day? Don't forget, Max's was a toy bike and he didn't ride that far in his life. You understand that you have to practice a lot before you can go that far." I replied calmly.

"You take kids side as if I am a child!" Lawrence exclaimed.

Under my breath "of course you are! You have to be told everything."

"I give up, seriously Lawrence, you have some work to do on yourself" and she just left.

Max has grown up feeling rejected and isolated by his father. Although Narissa felt she had a done a great job with him as a mother, she felt he needed the company of a male figure. He needed a mentor and someone to help him when he needed to shave his moustache and how to treat women and ways to deal with everyday life from a man's perspective.

She realised things turned bad when she started working on a regular basis on Saturdays. Max and the girls had no one to talk to. Narissa thought it was a great time for the children to bond with Lawrence. What she didn't realise is that Lawrence didn't want to, even though he said he did. He thinks kids are a menace. According to Lawrence kids have to be independent from the day they are born, well it seems that's what he means.

At 15 Max had a massive argument with Lawrence and it looked like he was going to punch Lawrence. The argument was started by Lawrence picking on Max for something real small. Lawrence doesn't know how to talk to children, won't listen, he judges them, he tells them off, threatens them and bullies them. He has never shown true love to the children. So Lawrence would continue an argument till he wins and if it looks like he is losing it he will become verbally and physically abusive.

'I guess Lawrence had a very different up bringing to mine. Lawrence was brought up in a very different way. His father was the head of the family and his mother never worked. She basically had to follow her husband who was the breadwinner of the family. His father was an angry man, being the eldest of 6 children he had a lot of responsibilities from a very early age.

However, when Narissa met Lawrence he showed no signs of dominating behaviour. He treated Narissa with respect and agreed with her ideas and everything seemed normal.

Every now and then she would just flip and scream at Lawrence for being so aloof. He used to tell her how his father would get mad with him for disappearing with his friends and his father never showed them love. His father worked hard for the family.

Lawrence thinks that his children use him for monetary gain. What else do the kids know? He was never around when they really needed him. Lawrence had always worked late and on weekends he would sit on his computer or the phone or the newspaper and never talk to anyone. Only time Lawrence would talk was when he had something bothering him, which usually means picking on something really small and has to be a family member.

At 16 Max was caught drinking alcohol with friends.

"Hey Narissa, we have some bad news," Nick called Narissa on her mobile phone, one of Max's really good friend from school. She felt that she knew already what he was going to say. Narissa got all quiet and her heart began to race. She knew it was Max. She could hear Lawrence shuffling the paper and moving around with heavy breathing, making his presence known in the house.

"What is it Nick?" Narissa asked worried but trying to keep it under her so Lawrence doesn't get to feel her anxiety. Narissa was half angry and half anxious.

"Well...Narissa, umm Max can't walk and he is very sick. Just don't ask anything yet. But can you come quickly please?"

She could sense the anxiety in Nick's voice and almost felt the nervousness in his voice.

"Yes, I am leaving home right away." She said very calmly.

She just picked the keys, her phone and wallet, when Lawrence appeared on the scene.

"What is it?" "I told you! That boy is up to no good! No one listens to me around here!" in a typical Lawrence panicky voice.

"I am going to pick up Max, he is sick." Narissa replied sternly.

"I want to come, mum." Ella is very concerned.

"Sure." I hugged Ella and glanced at Lawrence. "You can come if you promise not to say anything in the car. Don't make anything worse than it already is."

Max was going to a party organised by some boys in the year ahead of him. He had told Narissa about the party and also mentioned that there was going to be alcohol. He mentioned the names of all his friends going and Narissa felt good because his Asian friends were very responsible. Their parents were very strict and she knew they will all help each other.

20 minutes of driving and her heart was racing. In times like this Lawrence panics and takes all the long routes and gets lost. He knows where we have to go and has been to Matt's house before. He wanted to drive and Narissa let him just to avoid arguments. Lawrence seems to find something to argue about all the time.

As soon as the car was coming to a stop, Narissa jumped out, not waiting for the car to come to a complete halt. The security guy came up to the car but she didn't wait, she had to get to Max. She pushed her way through the gates, ignoring the second security guy and encountered a few of Max's friends from school, carrying beer cans.

"You guys have been drinking?" Narissa was alarmed.

"No not all of us, just some. Trust us, Max didn't drink." Said Nick.

"Then why is he sick and where is he?" Narissa was half angry and half sad.

'My baby! I want to cry but I have to be strong too. This is no time to get emotional or angry.' She thought.

She was ushered to the bench and there was Max, curled up on the bench, wet and smelly. The smell of sweat, dust and beer all around. He really looked like a homeless person.

"What do you mean he hasn't drunk?" She turned around to face his friends. She stayed calm but felt like yelling.

"He didn't drink beer. He was just having the fruit punch but some older kids had put other stuff in it." Nick explained.

"Where are the parents?" She asked.

"Oh, well Matt's dad is inside with his girlfriend. We are not allowed to go in." His friends all took turns to inform me what had happened. They had tried to push a lot of water down Max's throat and hence wet clothes.

They all helped her get Max into the car and Narissa sat at the back seat with him.

"Mumma, I didn't drink." Max is trying so hard to push words out of his mouth. His speech is slurry and with eyes half open, he looked a mass. His hair was all over his face and he couldn't sit up. She propped him up and held him up with the support of her shoulders. She couldn't smell beer on him.

"Mumma, I had fruit punch." Slurring his words out Max replied.

"I thought it was off but when I collapsed they told me it had spirits in it." Max managed to push some important information out.

"Don't talk right now. We are going home." I said to him pursing my lips.

They arrived home and Max didn't want to sleep in his bed. Throughout the journey home he kept telling Narissa how much he loved her and cared for her. He told her that he felt bad as couldn't talk to anyone as he was so wasted.

They managed to get him out of his wet polo shirt and pants and put some pyjamas on. He vomited once and kept saying "never again, never again."

Gosh. Narissa felt awful. She had given advice to her daughters about drinking at parties and date rapes and different types of drugs, not that they don't get enough advice at schools and social media. She was so thankful that her daughters were always cautious about this sort of stuff.

She suddenly felt so inadequate. 'Did I forget to mention all this to Max?' she thought.

He has heard Narissa talking to the girls and she just assumed that he knew.

'How do I talk to a boy about all this? I have told him but I guess not as seriously. Did I expect Lawrence to have done this? Doesn't Lawrence talk to him about all this 'stuff'?' Narissa couldn't help but question herself.

This incident made her realise that Lawrence has never talked to Max about anything in life. Although she provided the nurturing, the emotional support, she couldn't talk to him about boy 'stuff'. In other words Max has not ever been spoken to about being a young adult, by Lawrence.

'What have I done to my son? I feel broken today.' Narissa felt shattered.

She caressed his head with tears in her eyes. 'Why? What could I have done differently?' She thought.

Next morning, she started talking to Max and he just blabbed on about the fruit punch and then he couldn't remember much. Narissa and Ella told him about his behaviour the night before but he had no recollection.

Max had slept in Narissa's bed, had his arms tightly wrapped around her with legs spread across her body and sweating. At times she felt suffocated and pushed him aside but the whole night he wouldn't let go of her. She knew he needed a lot of love. Her heart felt so broken.

Lawrence as usual was furious. That is typical Lawrence. He wouldn't educate, warn or be involved but as soon as something happens, he is the first one to point a finger at someone and that is usually Narissa, the school, social media or the society.

Lawrence can't keep his negative thoughts inside. He has to execute everything that comes into his thoughts.

'A few years back she had taken him to see a coach who explained to Lawrence that some things were better left unsaid. She also gave Narissa a tip which was to give Lawrence some sort of a cue so that he will stop. That never worked. He was just really forceful.'

Lawrence had also been to see a Life coach, a lovely lady Narissa met through her work. Narissa had a session with her and she pretty much told her that she was on track with her life. That is when Narissa told her that she felt her drawback was her husband and Sally had suggested that Narissa sent him to see her. Narissa mentioned to Lawrence that it will help them to work together better as a family if he met with Sally just for one appointment. After the first session, Sally had re-booked him for 5 sessions and mentioned to Narissa that she since Lawrence didn't have a clue as to how to interact with children, Narissa could help him keep to his tasks.

'As if I hadn't known that! I have to keep him on task, like a mother?' she thought.

Lawrence had a tendency to just state the obvious. After his second session with Sally he came home and said he needed to spend one-to-one with each child and do something with them, anything that they enjoyed doing. Instead of just asking the children or suggesting he just told the children that he needed to do this. The children just looked at him in awe.

Of course Maddie thinks it is a bad idea because Lawrence wouldn't keep his promise. Max just shrugged his shoulders and said "stupid idea." Ella had no response.

'I thought that was a pretty lame thing to do. Didn't everyone do that?' thought Narissa.

It was obvious to Sally that Lawrence didn't do this and that's why she had suggested this to get him involved with the children and get to know them a bit better for the normal functionality of the family.

Narissa kept her mouth shut and thought it was ridiculous to have to teach someone to do this sort of thing. Surely people learn from experiences and grow. She always has to remind herself that Lawrence is all about himself.

'I look back all those years and realise that it was necessary for him to see this life coach.

Problem with this was, Maddie was 11, Ella was 6 and Max was

8, meaning they were able to understand a lot more than Lawrence thought. Lawrence came home feeling really happy with himself. Usually when he is happy the whole world has to be happy but when he goes in a downward spiral, everyone must stop and when he is down the world has to stop rotating. When he is happy he will come home bouncing and you can feel the exuberance of energy around him, he will be dancing his way, "guys, I have to spend a day in a week starting from this Saturday, with each one of you alone."

The kids all looked at him and went, "huh. What?"

Ella shook her head "dad, why? Are you going to die?"

Maddie had a smirk on her face, "maybe he is gay and wants us to know. Come out and just say it. We will all find out anyway, haha." The jokes that Maddie comes up with.

Max totally ignored him.

One look at Lawrence and Narissa thought obviously Sally forgot to mention that he should just do it and talk to each child separately, asking them what they would like to do this weekend and took them, one-by-one. Why does he have to make an announcement?

What a child he is.

All the children were so surprised and Maddie immediately declined. Ella said "um, no. Why would I want to do that?"

Max made a passing remark as he was leaving the room "how boring".

Oh shit! His ego has been crushed.

Maddie won't hold it and lashed out "dad, how can I trust you when you let me down so many times with the Karate lesson? How many times you took me late to school? How many times you took me to birthday parties late? How many times you made me miss my swimming class? No, thank you!"

Well, she is not wrong.

Ella is usually quiet but this time she felt a bit brave and spoke up "What will you do though? What do you mean spend time alone? Will you take me to a park and abandon me? Because I am not going."

She is right. Lawrence has a tendency to do that.

When Ella was 4 years of age we all went to Teddy bears picnic and Narissa had to disappear under the trees to feed Max. It was a hot day and she asked Lawrence to look after Maddie and Max. The trees were about 20 meters down the slope and the girls were busy watching the jester and enjoying fairy floss and ice creams. Max was always scared of the clowns and he was holding onto Lawrence when Narissa last saw him.

Narissa got Ella's food containers out and sat down on the picnic rug. It had barely been 5 minutes when she heard Maddie running down the slope screaming 'Mummy, mummy I want to go on the Ferris wheel".

"Maddie, where's dad? Ask him." Narissa retorted.

Just then she saw Lawrence appearing, but without Max.

She waited for a few seconds and didn't see Max at all. "Where is Max?" she asked questionably.

"I thought he was with you!" he exclaimed.

Sometimes you want to kill Lawrence. He really makes one boil.

"He was with you when I left you. He was holding onto you and I told you that I was leaving for the trees." Narissa was getting mad.

In this madness, Narissa forgot that she was feeding Ella and gave her extra mouthfuls which made her choke.

"Lawrence, go and freakin look for him NOW!" Narissa was totally mad, beyond her usual self. She was feeling nauseous and hot. It is a very hot day anyway. Narissa's fear of losing a child set her into panic mode.

Lawrence is frozen. He stands there not knowing what to do. Narissa got up and shoved the spoon into his hands, "you idiot! Feed Ella and I will go look for him."

She ran for her life and got Maddie to come with her. She didn't want Maddie to wander off. Lawrence cannot be trusted and we all know that. What annoys her is that Lawrence doesn't think it is anything to worry about.

Narissa ran around, calling for Max, with Maddie's help as

well. Maddie was very upset and she kept asking Narissa, what will happen if they didn't find him.

"Maddie, we will find him" Narissa kept reassuring her.

She suddenly saw the yellow shirt and brown shorts and knew that was Max. Narissa could only get a little glimpse of his tiny legs amongst all the crowd rushing around all the stalls. She tightened her grip on Maddie's hand and made her run as fast as possible in the direction she saw this little boy with similar colours to what Max was wearing. She just hoped and prayed to God that was Max. Her heart was racing and her breath was getting heavier. "I hope that is Max. I hope that is Max." She started calling out with a puffed voice. Narissa was getting emotional and her heart was pounding faster and faster and felt like it was going to take off.

"Mummy, don't worry. We will find him." Maddie told calmly.

'Gosh, Maddie is so sure of it. I should be too' Narissa reminded herself.

Narissa was pushing the crowd and apologising at the same time. People must have thought she was trying to get Maddie to the bathroom or something so they were good, everyone was making way. They got to the other side of this mad crowd and saw Max. Narissa couldn't hold her emotions any longer and she screamed out to Max, waving her arms frantically in excitement. She saw the look on Max's face and he looked terrified and didn't have a clue as to which direction to go.

Narissa gestured for him to stay where he was but he was trying too hard to get to her and Maddie. Narissa had to scream "Max stay where you are! We are coming!" To Maddie "C'mon Maddie, we need to hurry."

While running towards Max, Narissa had to keep her eyes on him in case he decides to run away in another direction to get to his mummy

The uneven ground made it difficult for Narissa to run fast especially while Maddie was hanging off her arms.

With tears in her eyes and feeling overwhelmingly exhausted

with emotions, Narissa kept moving fast. Max was way away on the other side and how long had he been wondering around scared, she didn't want to even think.

She was so glad to have him in her arms. "I am so sorry, baby."

She kissed him all over his head and hugged him so hard. Max held on to his mums' arms as if never to let go.

"Are you ok?" Maddie asked gently. She had her caring arms around Max. She cared very deeply for her little brother.

While walking back to the tree where Ella was sitting with Lawrence, Narissa asked Maddie what had happened and how Max got had lost them.

"Well, we were together and then we realised that dad was not with us. Max decided to find you, then I lost him." Maddie tried to explain.

Narissa was angry with Lawrence. This is not the first time either that he has been so irresponsible. She could just imagine what would have happened. Lawrence is a very selfish self-absorbed man and would have forgotten that he had the children with him. He might have been flirting with someone.

They arrived at the tree to where Ella and Lawrence were, only to find Ella screaming her heart out. Narissa asked Lawrence what had happened.

"Well, she was playing up and wouldn't eat so I gently smacked her."

"What?" I can't believe this. Didn't he think for a second that perhaps Ella was worried the way I had left? Maybe she wasn't hungry. What's the need to smack?

"You could have stopped feeding her. Maybe she didn't want to eat anymore." Narissa said with a disappointed voice.

Narissa doesn't understand Lawrence at all. She asked him again "why did you let the kids out of your sight?"

Again he replies "I thought they were with you." He looks down and Narissa knew he was lying. Three things that happen with Lawrence. He forgets that he has children and he has a responsibility and has been given a task or he found something more interesting or he was chatting with a woman. His biggest problem is that he always tries too hard to please other women.

'He once saw a pregnant women while we were standing in a cue for food at the food fair and Lawrence offered her my plate. I had gone out to get my dish and met up with Lawrence. I was standing in my cue for a while too but that didn't bother Lawrence. I was so mad and this lady just took my plate as if it was for free. Now that meant I had to go hungry. Lawrence wouldn't give his food away, but okay for him to give mine away. I actually didn't have a choice. He just took my plate off my hands and "Oh Hi, would you like this? Here, you can have this. It looks like this cue will take a while to move."

Yet 5 years later when I was pregnant and craving for KFC, Lawrence wouldn't stop the car for me to get a burger. Instead he teased me by driving around the roundabout making me crave more because of the strong smell and drove off. This kind of behaviour just doesn't make sense to me.'

He doesn't have a good relationship with his mother. They seem very detached. His mother is a very bossy woman and you cannot have a discussion with her. Her way or the high way! Lawrence obviously doesn't know the difference between a mother, a wife and other female he encounters. He gets so easily offended when Narissa tells him that she is not his mother.

One day she explained to him that a mother looks after her children, a wife is a partner that you work together with and you share duties, other females are people like any other males. He took offence. "Lawrence, I cannot mother you like your own mother did! For heavens sakes, I am your wife and your children's mother and I have the right to mother my own children. You are a father and your role has changed too. From a young boy to a man, a husband and now a dad."

"A real man loves his wife, puts his family as the most important thing in life. Being a good husband and a father brings peace and contentment."

# CHAPTER 18

TIRED OF ASKING Lawrence to help out Narissa decided to get a baby sitter to look after the children while she rushed off to work. Lawrence got home and he hated the fact that Narissa wasn't around. He yelled at the baby-sitter for letting the kids go wild. Apparently, they were all having fun, dancing on the coffee table in dress ups and make up. Maybe not a good idea to dance on the coffee table as it was Lawrence's favourite coffee table. He purchased it when they first bought a house, the black marble table together with the black marble dining table were the most expensive pieces of furniture he had bought. There were dirty plates and cups laying around the kitchen bench and the dining table.

He also yelled at the babysitter for her smelly socks. Lawrence can't hold his tongue and just blurbs out whatever comes to his mind. He doesn't give a hoot as to how his words might have an impact on someone's emotions and the worst part is he doesn't care. He embarrasses people and to tell her off in front of the children would have put her to shame.

If Narissa reminds him not to embarrass anyone like that, his answer is "well, I had to say it." She often reminds him to choose his time and place but he ignores her. Apparently he told Maxine off, 16 year old high school student for having smelly socks. Maxine left in a hurry when Narissa arrived home and she wondered what had happened. Maddie told her mum later that Lawrence had offended Maxine by telling her that her socks were smelly and she needed to wash them, she needed to be more hygienic. She could see how Maxine would have felt being told off in front of three young children. Poor Maxine would lose all dignity with the children. 'Well I have lost yet another helper.' Thought Narissa, thanks to her up himself husband.

When Narissa is home she is expected to have a show home. She has e to frantically tidy, clean, keep children under control and everything has to be in its place. Yet, Lawrence is not a tidy person himself. He is the most disorganised person you will come across. All the bills, statements and important papers will be splashed around in the study as if a tornado had been through. Magazines, newspapers and flyers will be thrown around on the dining table, coffee table, lamp table, bedside tables and any other shelf space you can see and think of. If there is space on the buffet table he manages to fill it up. If Narissa asks him to tidy up as things are getting out of control he looks at her as if to say it is not his job. She asked the kids to separate the library books from their own books one day. Normally the kids own books stay on shelves and the library books stay in the library bag, three bags with each of the 3 children's names embroidered on them, her own ingenuity. Somehow they got mixed up. Maddie and Ella did what they could but when she went through Max's bag she found his own favourite book in it which made Narissa think that perhaps she should look through other books as well. Since she was flat out with other chores, she asked Lawrence to do this small task to help her out. Thinking this was a small job which he could do while sitting and watching TV. He didn't have to move or talk to anyone, as he cannot talk to anyone in his house. "They are not my books and I don't have to do this job." Came his pathetic reply.

Narissa just clenched my teeth and left the room. Another little chore she will have to remember before the school pick up next day. She always got the children to help her out but sometimes it was easier to do these little tasks while they were all in bed. This way no one will ask to read her a book.

So tired of getting Lawrence involved in anything to do with the family. Sometimes she wants to shake his head and ask him if he actually understands what it means to run a house and be actively involved with the family.

Narissa picked up some books from the library herself regarding self-healing. She read quietly in bed and could relate to her own life. The grief, hurt, feeling of isolation was all becoming part of this relationship. She could maintain her mental health very well learning from the self-help books.

Her books became her best companion.

"Selfish people cannot understand what it means to maintain a relationship, neither will they ever see why it is necessary to do so."

# CHAPTER 19

*"Young people are in a condition like permanent intoxication,
because youth is sweet and they are growing."— Aristotle*

THE KIDS ARE all grown up and in their teenage years. There's only two way things can go. Either they will all turn out really outlaw or be nerdy.

Maddie is very independent now and after years of fighting with her dad, she has decided to focus on her career. Narissa is so proud of her angel. She is studying law at University and really wants to get into the justice system helping out with legal issues surrounding domestic violence, children who go wayward and she is really passionate about her work.

Max cannot decide what he wants to do. Max has gone into a deep depression a few times and so has Ella.

Narissa sits back and thinks if she had done things differently, what would life had been like.

The years of her own turmoil is taking its toll on her. She has aching joints at age 50, she has stomach issues and has been warned as she could develop stomach cancer.

She has taken the children to Psychologists, healers including Channel healing, Reiki and Theta healing. She has truly run out of avenues for self-healing etc.

She bit the bullet and went to see a Marriage Counsellor who very clearly pointed out that Narissa was not looking at the root cause of her problems and her children's issues. She had been applying the band aid effect which clearly wasn't working. The root cause of the problem was Lawrence. She had to convince him to get counselling or move out.

With Lawrence working late every night, Narissa trying to pursue her own interests especially regarding her career, was not easy. The emotional ups and downs of the children were not dealt with very well. Lawrence who never took time to understand his wife or his children became a stranger to all. He had anger problems for a very long time and wouldn't listen when Narissa advised him to get some professional help. He thought he didn't have a problem.

"It is not normal Lawrence, to be angry at little things." She explained to him.

Lawrence didn't believe her and continued his way of verbally abusing everyone. He made promises he couldn't keep, he would not communicate with everyone at home but continued to be the controlling figure.

Narissa started up her beauty salon but only lasted a couple of years. Every Thursday she had to work late nights and Saturday she had to open the shop till 5. She had an assistant but it wasn't an ideal situation for Lawrence. He wanted Narissa home.

On Thursdays she would ask Lawrence to help the children with homework or anything in the house, Lawrence would rather be out with 'the boys'. He told Narissa that he was working.

One day she had to rush home when Ella decided to end her life. Lucky Narissa had a cancellation and drove home speedily when Max called to say Ella was hysterical. Narissa found Lawrence having a massive argument with Ella who was standing with a knife in her hand. Not a situation Narissa had hoped to see.

After she diffused the situation she got to the bottom of it and discovered that Ella had wanted to go out and Lawrence was trying to stop her because she had already been out on a Friday night. Lawrence wanted her to stay home.

Narissa was furious at the way he was carrying on and being unreasonable. Lawrence refuses to see Ella's point of view.

Sure Ella had been out on a Friday night with a group of friends but she told Narissa of her whereabouts as usual. Ella was going out on Saturday with a different lot of friends to a birthday party.

Lawrence couldn't see that. If he said no, then he will make sure that he sticks with the no, at all cost.

Whole reason Maddie became a hermit. Maddie couldn't go out with her friends and because of all the verbal abuse she suffered from Lawrence, Maddie just stopped going out altogether and became absorbed in her studies and work. She loved her netball and spent her weekends playing and some nights of training. She didn't have much of a social life.

Narissa realised it was important for Ella to get a job so she could be out of Lawrence's face. She could help out at Narissa's salon but that meant Ella would have to work for peanuts. Ella didn't like the idea and eventually managed to find a job at a retail outlet. She took as many shifts as possible during her university breaks and whatever she could fit in during semester time.

Narissa in the end sold the salon as it was getting too hard for her to manage the family and work commitment. Her salon had really taken off and she had repeat business which meant she was booked all Saturday and Thursday evenings plus the school hours she was working. Without any help from Lawrence, she single handily was juggling a lot.

Max had football training during the week days and Maddie had netball training. Ella played hockey and it was all too much for Narissa, especially when she wasn't allowed to buy takeaways or have a cleaner. Narissa made a lot of sacrifices and often feeling like a solo parent.

She was relieved to have sold her salon but very disappointed at the same time because she loved her work and the interaction with her clients. She cried when she handed her keys to the salon to the new business owner. The new business owner could see what the business meant for Narissa and she offered to employ her on either casual basis or fixed few days. Narissa's clients were not happy either and she was undulated with gifts, cards and tears.

Narissa stayed home and felt useless again. She was running the children everywhere, cooking, cleaning and had to find something to do for herself. She started swimming lessons on a Tuesday evening. One evening she had free, that is after picking kids from school, feeding them, minding their homework and then she could take off. Some days Max didn't want to eat when Narissa left so she got him organised with the homework and had made arrangements with Lawrence to come home by at least 6.30 or 7pm to finish off where they left.

Eventually, the swimming lessons had to be stopped because Narissa discovered that Lawrence arrived home usually 10 minutes before her, which was close to 9pm. Lawrence made excuses when Narissa asked him why he couldn't be home just that one night a week. He told her it was his expanse claim night and the computer at work has a bigger screen and it is easier for him to work on that then at home.

Total lies! As soon as Narissa gave her swimming lesson, Lawrence started coming home at a reasonable time. The expanse claim day had changed?

Narissa was feeling more and more helpless. Every time she suggested that they went out for a meal or to movies, Lawrence claimed to have no money. He demanded to get the money from the sale of Narissa's business to be put into the mortgage account.

Often Narissa stayed up all night trying to figure out what was going on. Was she insane? Why was Lawrence treating her in this manner?

Max had fallen behind in school work, Ella was struggling and Maddie was no different. Max and Ella both had private tuition and Maddie just had to spend extra time with her studies. Finally Narissa got the kids back on track with their studies.

Lawrence was a lot happier once Narissa became a stay at home mum again, which was not Narissa's desire at all. Lawrence had the house immaculate, clothes washed and dinner cooked.

Narissa tried to talk to Lawrence about setting up her salon at home but Lawrence wouldn't hear of it. She argued with him for days but he won't budge.

One day feeling very hurt, Narissa was lying on her bad when Max entered the room. Max started talking about his future plans when he picked up Lawrence's phone and showed her a picture of Lawrence with some woman.

"Mum, do you know this lady?" He asked.

Narissa had a look and she felt even worse. She was never the jealous type but that picture was a slap on her face. Lawrence was sitting on a bench with arms wrapped around this woman.

"I haven't seen this lady before, Max. She must be someone from his work." Narissa replied showing no feelings at all.

After a while they found more pictures with different women and young girls. Max left without saying much while Narissa was feeling lumps in her throat.

She was wondering if that was the reason Lawrence had been working late, if that was the reason why he called her wrinkly and aged. Lawrence just out of the blue made a comment at Narissa that she was getting wrinkles and that she was putting on weight.

She couldn't help but wonder if Lawrence was having an affair. He had once told her after an argument that he had a lot of opportunities, meaning he had a lot of women chasing him. He also told her that he was looking very young for his age.

What an ego, Narissa had thought at that time.

The picture on his phone began to bug her. She couldn't help herself so approached Lawrence that night.

"Why are you on my phone? Who gave you permission? You were snooping? You don't trust me? Do you? Do you?" He barked at her and trying to push her on the bed.

"Lawrence! Stop! I have the right to know! I am your wife!" Narissa screamed. She was sure the kids had heard.

"What were you doing on my phone?" He asked again as if she had committed a crime.

"You gave Max your phone to see the Spotify music and that's when he showed me the photo." Narissa cried out.

What really made Narissa even angrier is the fact that Lawrence snoops and checks her messages all the time. As soon as her phone beeps he picks it up to see.

She expected Lawrence to show her the photos and talk about it. Instead he made this into a different argument. It has become all about someone snooping on his phone.

Next minute, he went into the shower taking his time, came out and said he had diarrhoea and spent time in the toilet. Then he sat on the bed and went through the pictures saying he can't find any photos.

Narissa knew he had deleted them and she knew how to get the recently deleted photos on but he pushed her and tried to bully her by saying she had no right to snoop into his phone.

Narissa would never forget this incident. It out another mark on her heart like a knife slicing a part of it. She couldn't sleep that night and yet Lawrence complained about work and went to sleep.

Narissa asked him again a few months later. His story changed. He told her that someone had taken the picture on his phone.

"Am I that stupid, Lawrence?" She asked.

"I am asking you about the lady in the photo with you holding her as if she was your possession. I just asked you about this woman and who she was. You are making excuses." She replied.

"I don't know her name!" He screamed at her.

"Then how come you are sitting with her like she is your girlfriend?" Narissa asked again.

"What's with you? Why can't you let it go!" Lawrence barked at her.

"Why should I? I am your wife and have a right to know!" Narissa screamed.

"Look, I told you I don't know what you are talking about." Lawrence marched off.

Shabina

Now that her children are older and Narissa has more time she can really get to the bottom of this. She didn't want him to get away with this especially since she had in the past. He saw that as her weakness and overrode her. Narissa wasn't going to anymore.

Few months later she asked him again. "Lawrence, I cannot go on living under the same roof as you if you cannot be honest with me. I want you to be honest with me. I need some answers for myself so I can understand myself."

"What do you want to know?" He screamed at her.

"Please stop screaming. Kids are all trying to sleep. I have tried to take you out so we can discuss our relationship. You refuse to be seen with me. I am not comfortable with you working late like this. You smell of pub and I know you have been drinking. Your eyes turn red whenever you have been out drinking. I want to know why you lie to me about working late. Why can't you honestly tell me that you went out instead of telling me that you were working? I also want you to tell me about this woman in the picture on your phone that you deleted the night I asked you." Narissa asked him politely.

Lawrence turned wild. "Why do you keep pestering me? I haven't done anything wrong! For heavens sakes, what do you want from me?" He screamed so loud as if he would strangle her right now.

"Lawrence, I am asking you because you have never answered me properly. Don't you think I need to know?" She asked.

"We were at this fundraiser but I don't know the woman. She had dreadlocks or something. I don't know her name. I told you my friend took the picture and he used my phone." He replied.

"First time I asked you, your response was different. Now you know which picture I am talking about? The truth, Lawrence. That's what I am after." She put it firmly.

"Do you believe in God? Do you believe in the power of truth?" She asked.

"I told you! I didn't do anything wrong!" He screamed again.

"What is with you telling me that you haven't done anything wrong? Let me be the judge of that. Why can't you tell me what you

238

were doing with this woman cuddling her like your girlfriend? If your friend took a picture on his phone then I wouldn't have known about it?" She asked angrily.

Lawrence can't see what Narissa's problem is.

"I think we need to go for counselling because you are not understanding me. You think I have no right to understand why you would be holding anyone like that." Narissa pointed out.

"I don't see the need for counselling. There isn't anything wrong with me and I haven't done anything wrong or done anything to put you to shame." He replied.

"Don't you want to sort this out for me?" She asked feeling hurt.

"There's nothing to tell. I have work in the morning and I have an early start." He replied.

Lawrence just went off to bed and when Narissa went to bed an hour later, he was sitting on his phone. 'So much for an early start.' She thought. She didn't say anything because she didn't want to upset him because he will make her life misery.

Narissa knows from previous experience what early starts mean for Lawrence. He goes for breakfasts with work mates and as she found out another time, Lawrence was meeting his female boss who had lost her husband in a fatal car crash and needed a shoulder to cry on. Lawrence provided her his shoulders, instead of taking kids to school when the school was just around the corner from his work.

Lawrence was always running off to work early like 6.30am and latest by 7am but as soon as Narissa sold her salon, he started going to work later. He wasn't leaving home till 8 or 8.30 and sometimes working from home.

'Why couldn't he do this when I needed help? I had pleaded so many times but he blatantly refused telling her he had important meetings.' Narissa thought.

She wasn't stupid though. She knew he was avoiding responsibility and wanted her to run the kids to school and made himself look very important. How could someone not know what Lawrence is up to?

Maddie became Lawrence's scapegoat. She was a feisty character by nature and won't tolerate any form of abuse so she stood up for herself and reminded Narissa that she was weak. Narissa didn't like that so kept getting stronger by seeing healers and Homeopathy. Lawrence behaves very unreasonably even in public and argues with Maddie or starts yelling at Narissa if things are not going his way which makes Maddie even more mad.

When Narissa tried to tell Lawrence to keep boardroom stuff at home, he screamed at her "People should see what Maddie is like!"

"Why? What is your problem? Don't you ever think that people might think what kind of a father you are treating your daughter with disrespect?" She asked.

"It's not me! Clearly children misbehave and we have to punish them. They have to do as their fathers tell them." He replied.

Lawrence went on to tell his family that his daughter suffered from mental illness, yet Maddie was never diagnosed. When Narissa took her to the developmental Psychologist, he had explained that Maddie had some anxiety issues but not any other mental health issues. The anxiety was because of Lawrence's parenting because Maddie was not like that in her younger years. The family and friends all commented that Maddie was a bright intelligent girl and a very future thinker. 'What happened to her?' everyone used to ask.

Ella became the favourite child. She would keep quiet whenever Lawrence yelled at her and she would never argue with him. On the surface she looked like she was fine but she hated the arguments, name calling, controlling father and lack of support from Lawrence. She had huge self- esteem issues, she didn't believe in herself and yet was very pretty and bright young girl.

Max couldn't find any peace within himself for a while. He didn't like the school because he had a lot of learning gaps and his inner turmoil ate his soul.

According to Lawrence Narissa was to be blamed for this. She should never have gone to work.

"A guy is only insecure about losing his girl when he knows that someone else can treat her better" —*Kushandwizoom*

# CHAPTER 20

*"A person who never learned to TRUST confuses intensity with Intimacy, obsession with care and control with security"* —Anon

How to really live with a Narcissistic person?

A NARCISSISTIC PERSON IS not only focussed on themselves, their appearance and their own interests but they can never really understand anyone. They refuse to acknowledge that someone else might have feelings and desires. They forget to see other people around them besides themselves. They think their way is the correct way and fail to see the other side of the coin. They will never back down from an argument. They will chase something because they wanted it, then it becomes an obsession and if they can't get it then they might either play the victim or they will become abusive in a verbal or physical way.

Living with a Narcissistic personality is an art, a life-long learning experience if you are up with the challenge. Life can be up and down and while you are yo-yoing around, feel bruised and battered and sometimes happy, you are always alone. You will always be unsupported and you will never know where you stand. The children will suffer because they will always be thrown in the deep end, with no emotional support, always made to feel guilty, no guidance and always deprived of feeling loved.

Learning to live with someone who is totally focussed on themselves takes a lot of effort physically and emotionally. Most people will see a side that is totally different to your experience at home. The hurt, deceits, lies and put downs can only be tolerated by a few. Most people would give up on a relationship. It is difficult when children are involved.

A person with NPD will always have a scapegoat and a golden child. The scapegoat will always be made to feel inadequate and the golden child will feel they are the chosen ones.

So what happens in these relationships is usually the victim, if I may say is the one who puts up with the put downs, gets the blame, usually decides to quit this relationship. This might seem easy but the person with NPD will feel like he/she is the victim in this case. This usually makes it a challenging scenario. Most often, I have seen women who have put up with all the abuse are often either very friendly, I mean unusually friendly or very timid. The friendly ones realise that they cannot cope anymore and need to have a break. The timid ones generally feel very guilty of calling the relationship off or even discussing with anyone.

The victimising partner, who feels they haven't done 'anything' wrong will take off and leave their partners high and dry. Sometimes they will buy you out if you have a property together and everything you own or have shared together, becomes theirs, the victimising partner. Either way, you will end up with much less than you have given.

Can Counselling or Psychologist help? It can help if the person labelled with NPD is willing to accept that they need help and wants the partnership/marriage to work. Most often these people simply don't care. Since they don't have the ability to empathise, they will continue life as if nothing has happened. Most likely scenario is they (NPD) will find a new partner and will carry on as if they have been very severely damaged by their previous marriage/relationship.

They will act their best and will shower their new partners with everything they didn't in the first marriage /relationship. They will do everything that their previous partner would have indicated that they wanted to do with life and in life and that includes travelling, buying a car, house or whatever it is. They become very competitive. They will show that they are the happiest without their previous relationship.

Some of the other therapies that have really been effective are more along the lines of Reiki, Spiritual healing or even Homeopathy. They all require a lot of commitment from the person suffering with NPD. The commitment is not usually a strong element in a NPD. They often give up after one or two sessions. They need encouragement, support and more often the coaching from their partners or the therapist they are seeing.

How do you truly live with a person with NPD?

The only most effective way is to avoid all arguments which isn't always a healthy option. Sometimes discussions are required in a family or relationship. Avoidance? Perhaps, avoidance is the best single method. This means living your own single life but with a partner who is only physically there. So the point of being in this relationship is?

There is no easy solution and therefore, in my experience it is better to walk away from this relationship as early as possible. Damaging yourself and the children is not worth all the effort. It is very much a form of domestic violence and not always easy to prove as there may not be any form of visible physical abuse.

To all the parents who read this book, I would like you to understand that if you have a son or a daughter who exhibits these traits, get help soon and make sure you stay with them mentally and emotionally till they have learnt who they really are inside.

Few lessons here in this story that are so deep that they will hurt a wounded soul. A relationship can be maintained if there is an understanding, compromise, respect, value and a bit of self-pride but above all... true love. If you only take time to understand another's view point, show empathy, feel compelled to be the emotional support person, you know they care, you know that is love.

Love is blind for sure. What attracts us to someone? Sometimes it is pure lust but you know quite quickly that is not true love. As soon as the lust is over the connection fizzles out, just like opening a bottle of fizzy. The taste is fantastic while the fizz is there. As soon as the fizz is gone the drink is tasteless.

Opposites attract and is that a good mix for a marriage?

You come together for a reason and perhaps the lessons in life have been learnt and it is time to move on. What are the lessons in life?

The lessons are the karmic patterns that we have acquired not by choice but by birth. We come into this world, to a family where we

Why is change so difficult for some people? Why change in some cultures is seen to a bad action?

Change is vital for growth, for mental growth, for physical growth and for human beings to evolve. Mental emotional growth happens when a mind is open to change. Growth is absolutely necessary to acknowledge the change. In some cultures there is very little acknowledgement of mental growth. When a child is born, the parents focus on the well-being of their child mostly in regards to physical growth. A child develops from a baby to toddler to a young boy/girl, then to a young adult, an adult and then maybe into parenthood and all the physical changes comes with this growth.

This growth should also be looked at in terms of mental and emotional growth as the phases move. Nothing is static, energy must move and shift. As the changes happen at the mental/emotional level we see a baby growing into toddler stage where they learn to crawl or walk, their awareness grows and with this this growth we see physical changes. The mental/emotional growth continues and as the toddlers enter the young boy/girl state you see many changes, many emotional states and all this time the parents are growing with their children, learning the survival skills in life.

As young adults, do parents continue to mother their children? The answer is no. A young adult needs space, they feel the need for independence, and they want to venture out to the bigger wider world. Do they stop growing?

They do not stop growing because the mental/emotional state is still growing from all the experiences. This stage of a young adult's life is absolutely important. They will make mistakes, they are bound to experiment with life and because they have had good solid foundation at home, they will always maintain their elements of respect, value and foresights in their clear vision.

However, if a child has been wrapped in cotton wool, over protective mothering, parents who haven't allowed them to develop at their own pace, they have been bound by social constraints, they will develop deep psychological wounds. These children can develop all sorts of problems in their young adult years. The mental health issues can become more prominent during this phase. How they deal with problems, how they react to adversity, how they interact with their peers, their attitude to life, people and to the rest of the world will take shape in undesirable ways.

In a Narcissistic personality disorder, this person will have no problem solving skills, no set boundaries, they cannot see the future, they will conform to please others to get attention, to get ahead, they will travel through life in a haphazard away, they will blame the rest of the world for their misfortune, for their lack of achievement, they will never find peace within themselves as they are always looking outward. They feel there are greener pastures elsewhere. In a marriage they may be married to the most beautiful woman/ man in the world but they will always be on the lookout for another. They want to know that they are wanted, that everyone desires them. They feel as though they are the most important people in the world, have the best house, car and all the material wealth in the world. They have to constantly prove to the world that they are the most important people in the world.

They will bend over backwards in a workplace hoping to get a raise, or a better position. They will not give up till they will have what they put their minds to. They are rigid, they are full of anxiety, insecurities, lacking empathy but they will never show their vulnerable side to people until and unless there is a reward at the end.

The reward, recognition and praise will drive them to the point of exhaustion but they will not give up, because they are right and they know best.

A person with this disorder is very childlike and that's why they have to have their own way. They will fight to have their way because their parents didn't deal with their tantrums in an age appropriate way in the toddler years.

The child will look for the mother in terms of stress so when push comes to shove they will hurt the people closest to them without knowing what they are doing or how they are impacting their relationships with the loved ones.

They would have suffered rejection from a parent and can become aggressive when angry. They may have been treated as kings or queens of the house and parents gave in to all their demands, all their needs have always been met and they cannot take rejection well, they cannot take disappointment well and they will not accept 'no' for an answer, yet they are happy to reject their own loved ones, disappoint them and most of all say 'no' to their loved ones most often than they will say 'yes'.

Their partners and children soon learn not to approach them for anything but at the same time they will experience rejection and abuse, their energy will be drained due to the unnecessary arguments and yet they will be helpless to move on. If they move away, they are bad and if they stay they are bad. You can't live and you can't leave. Most times you will find the children of this sort will develop a whole lot of chronic diseases that all stem from the autoimmune system like thyroid problems, diabetes, depression and many other ailments.

"Accept the children the way we accept trees—with gratitude, because they are a blessing—but do not have expectations or desires. You don't expect trees to change, you love them as they are." — Isabel Allende

# CHAPTER 21

*"Putting yourself first is not selfish. Thinking*
*about yourself constantly is."—Anon*

What makes a person Narcissistic?

NARISSA HAS BENT over backwards to keep the family together. She has fulfilled Lawrence's needs, been there for him in bad times and good times which have not been many. Every time she tries to think of a good time, she remembers all the arguments that went with it. This cancelled all the good times.

Narissa has realised one thing that all the time she had been verbally abused was not her fault. Although in the early years of her relationship she felt that she was responsible for Lawrence's happiness and always blamed herself. She took a lot of therapy to keep herself in shape especially her mental health.

Maddie reminded Narissa that she had done some papers in Psychology and profiled her dad with her lecturer who told Maddie that her father had serious issues. That's when Maddie started hassling Narissa to divorce her husband and make a better life for herself. Narissa couldn't think of leaving because she felt that no one would employ her, getting her registrations will be too difficult and she was too old to start all over again.

Ella suddenly came up with the idea that she wanted to be a Psychologist because of all the mental health issues surrounding her home. Suffering from eating disorders, psychological disorders she wanted to understand what caused mental illness in people and be help to people who actually suffered from them.

Narissa can't blame them. She had been to a healer a long time ago who told Narissa that Lawrence had deep wounds to deal with and till he acknowledges and deals with them he will never be able to love anyone. When push comes to shove he will always blame Narissa. On the other hand, Narissa believed in the power of positive thinking and truly believed that with her love she could turn it all around and help Lawrence.

Lawrence on the other hand didn't give anyone any love back and always thought he deserved more than others.

He pretended to understand Narissa and was willing to help himself in order to be a more connected father to his children. He will promise to help himself and play the sympathy card. Narissa often believed him but then there was no follow up. When asked he will make excuses and tell her work was really busy.

After years of trying Narissa decided to give up and concentrate on herself. This of course is not what Lawrence wanted. He wants Narissa to be with him so he could use her, abuse her and control her. That gave him a sense of importance.

What made Narissa tip over is when she found out about his lies. The more she began to force Lawrence to talk the more she realised his lies were too much for her to handle. The late night working, coming home at 10, 11 or 3 am, it wasn't all work. He had been out and then went back to work. Sometimes he went out and played pool. Sometimes he just went clubbing. He was always eager to please others and be liked by everyone.

When his mother left the family for another man, which was 32 years ago, Lawrence was devastated. He went to Narissa's work and had a meltdown. Narissa realised afterwards that he was feeling bad about himself that his mother had left him. Who would care for him? He felt abandonment, he felt betrayed, and he felt a huge loss. He didn't really care if his mother had made a mistake and weather she was going for good reasons. It wasn't about his mother at all. It was all about himself.

When Lawrence lost his job he blamed the company. He was devastated and blamed Narissa for stopping him from working late and long hours, not that he had listened anyway. He blamed everyone as if it was the end of the world. It took a lot out of Narissa who was juggling so much already. She basically had to become a counsellor because Lawrence wouldn't visit one himself.

He wouldn't support Narissa at home so she could work and yet was ready to call her names and tell her she was a user, she was living off him and she didn't care about his grief.

All the sacrifices Narissa made for the sanity of her family just goes up like smoke, burnt to ground because Lawrence is unable to see her contribution. Lawrence thinks he has worked really hard for the family when in fact he had been chasing money instead of thinking about the best outcomes for the family.

Lawrence was happy complaining about kid's expenditure but never offered to help them find part time work or work on their CV's.

Narissa had taken the time to teach the children to drive and helped them get their licences so they could be more mobile. Lawrence had never taken the time to help out.

He absolutely hated Ella and Max going out at night to clubs or partying and to catch trains back home but never offered to drive them to their destinations or to pick them up.

Narcissist manipulate situations and pretend that they don't know what's happening. It is a bizarre situation when they blast their family with hurtful words and then walk away as if nothing has happened. Instead they feel the other person did the wrong and got punished. Punishment is a big part of narcissistic behaviour. They feel every wrong doer has to be punished.

The bottom line is for the Narcissist person it is all about themselves. When the real Lawrence presented himself to Narissa she was very scared. At the same time she felt sorry for Lawrence. She felt stuck in between 2 hard rocks.

All Narissa ever wanted in a marriage was a long term friend and all she got was a lonely, controlling sad man who didn't know how to be someone's friend.

Narissa thought she was a lot smarter at picking her partner in life than she had done. After refusing a proposal where she felt suffocated in the relationship after a while, she vowed to never marry someone who didn't allow her to be herself. Maybe karma got her. Maybe she should have asked for what she was wanting and not what she didn't want.

How could she have been so blind?

What makes a person into a Narcissistic individual is a series of deep seated grief, hurt and feeling of separation. They hide their real selves and that's why they go flirting with everyone to make themselves feel better; they go splash out on workmates to show they are rich; they continue to lie and make up stories and then they lose the truth. They don't know what is real anymore. To mask all of these feelings they want to show the world that they have a lot of money, they have the best of everything, they have a lovely family yet, the family have experienced totally opposite to all this. The image that is portrayed to the world is far from reality. The family have suffered for years and they all run out of energy to defend themselves.

A Narcissistic individual is a very lonely person. They are lucky if someone has stayed with them long enough to have children and make it through without being damaged themselves.

"A Narcissist would rather impress a stranger than to love his own family"

When the mask drops

Life's journey meanders through
With thorns and Roses abound
Heart that was red feels blue
Chest filled heavily crowned
Numbness prevails as if death is near

Despite my selfless love
My generosity lacked steering
Habitual creatures of love
Created tears with no meaning
Numbness prevails as if death is near

The hours spent alone at dining table
The hours spent alone in bed with coldness
The yearning for that hug of sable
Never arrives despite all the baldness
Numbness prevails as if death is near

Marriage vows lost their meaning
When life's challenges took over
Promises made were freezing
As the long road to happiness soured
Numbness prevails as if death is near

The reality of who we became
Because of the differences too vast
Suddenly feeling alone with shame
Made it difficult to grasp
Numbness prevails as if death is near

The meaning of life
The honesty of love
The happiness of living
The giving in love
Is far from reality
Numbness prevails as if death is near